The Allergy-Free Cookbook

The Allergy-Free Cookbook

DAIRY FREE GLUTEN FREE
WHEAT FREE EGG FREE
NO ADDED SUGAR

Michelle Berriedale-Johnson

Thorsons
An Imprint of HarperCollins*Publishers*

Thorsons
An Imprint of HarperCollins*Publishers*
77–85 Fulham Palace Road
Hammersmith, London W6 8JB

5 7 9 10 8 6

Originally published as
Sainsbury's Special Diets Cookbook by
HarperCollins*Publishers* 1995
Published by Thorsons 1999

© Michelle Berriedale-Johnson

Michelle Berriedale-Johnson asserts the moral right
to be identified as the author of this work

A catalogue record for this book is
available from the British Library

ISBN 0 7225 3878 2

Printed in Great Britain by
Clays Ltd, St Ives plc

Contents

About the Author

Having spent all her professional career in the food business, first as a caterer and then as a journalist and food writer, Michelle became interested in special diets when her small son was diagnosed as being dairy intolerant. Following her experiments with soya as an alternative to dairy milk, she started a food company manufacturing a soya-based ice cream. a range of vegetarian 'ready meals', excluding dairy foods, gluten, eggs and fat, plus a range of dairy-free chocolate novelties. Michelle now runs a magazine about dietary problems. She lives with her son, Jonathan, in north London.

Note to the Reader

Before following the dietary advice given in this book, readers are urged to give careful consideration to the nature of their particular health problem and to consult a competent physician if in any doubt.

Introduction

The first thing to realise about food allergies is that a genuine food allergy – when the body reacts in an immediate, dramatic and even fatal way to a food – is quite rare. What most people suffer from is food intolerance or sensitivity. This can make you feel unwell – very unwell if it goes undiagnosed for a long time – but only in the most extreme cases can it be fatal.

In true food allergy a certain food (such as peanuts) causes an immediate chemical reaction in the body. It is very rare for such a condition to improve so the allergic person will always need to avoid that food.

A food intolerance or sensitivity is when the body has difficulty in coping with a certain food or group of foods. This can be caused by the temporary (or permanent) lack of a certain chemical, normally an enzyme, which enables the digestion to break down and absorb the food. Alternatively the digestive system and especially its lining (the gut wall) may have been damaged, allowing undigested particles of food or proteins to escape from the gut into the blood stream. Once they reach the blood stream they may cause any number of 'allergic' reactions.

It is possible, although rare, to be born with either of these conditions. Far more often they will arise as a result of an illness, infection, trauma or stress. All of these conditions also weaken the immune system, thereby reducing the body's ability to cope with 'foreign' food particles invading its bloodstream. The resulting 'allergic' reaction will then put further stress on the system.

If either the 'sensitivity' or the underlying digestive problem goes undiagnosed for any length of time the extra stress on the system will debilitate that person further – and there is a good chance that the number of foods which cause a reaction will grow. In really serious cases there may be very little left that the sufferer can eat without causing an adverse reaction.

Of course it follows therefore that if the underlying health problems can be resolved, the chances are that the digestive system will largely return to normal and the food sensitivities disappear.

Symptoms of Food Intolerance

One of the frustrating things about food intolerance is that both its causes (the specific foods) and its symptoms can be almost infinitely varied. However, certain food groups – usually foods that are consumed in large quantities – and related symptoms are relatively common.

Dairy Intolerance

Dairy intolerance can be a reaction either against the lactose sugar in milk or against the milk's proteins.

A lactose intolerance arises when the body manufactures insufficient lactase enzyme to digest the lactose. Although permanent lactase deficiency is rare, a temporary deficiency after a stomach upset or a bout of diarrhoea is quite common, especially in babies. Withdrawing the lactose from the diet for even just a few weeks will often allow the lactase enzyme to re-colonise the bowel, thereby solving the problem. In more serious cases the lactose may need to be withdrawn on a long-term basis.

Symptoms of dairy intolerance often include colic in babies. Older children and adults are more likely to experience vomiting, breathing problems (asthma and hay fever), ear, nose and throat problems (runny nose, blocked ears, sore throat) and skin eruptions (spots, eczema etc.).

Those who cannot take cow's milk can often tolerate goat's and sheep's milk. Cow's milk, cheese and yoghurt can also be acceptable to people with relatively mild lactose intolerance as the lactose has been all but eliminated, or converted into less allergenic lactic acid in the processing.

Coeliac Disease and Wheat Intolerance

These are among the most trying intolerance to deal with since not only do gluten and wheat starch form an intrinsic part of staple foods such as bread, but they are used, if only in small quantities, in an enormous number of manufactured products.

Gluten intolerance or Coeliac disease is not, strictly speaking, an intolerance but an autoimmune disease and therefore unlikely to be cured. The gluten damages the villi or little fronds lining the digestive tract thus preventing the sufferer from absorbing any nutrition. In wheat intolerance the body reacts to proteins in the wheat – often, in the western world, because we eat too much of it.

Because gluten and wheat starch are so widely used as manufacturing or processing aids and because so many of our staple carbohydrate foods (bread, cakes, biscuits, pasta, pizza etc.) are wheat based, it is difficult to avoid.

Both gluten and wheat intolerance can cause diarrhoea, pain, bloating, weight loss and general malaise. In babies they may also cause pale, foul smelling stools, wind and bloating which normally develop a few weeks after cereals are introduced. If untreated they can cause damage to the gut wall, which, in turn, can make the sufferer more prone to react badly to other foods.

Egg Intolerance
Symptoms of egg intolerance can also be very varied but usually include skin problems (eczema or 'nettle rash'), vomiting and diarrhoea and, sometimes, asthma.

Soya Intolerance
With the increased consumption of soya in the west, so soya intolerance is growing. Again symptoms vary but are usually digestive – vomiting, bloating, pain, diarrhoea etc.

Nuts
Potentially fatal, allergy to nuts has been growing over the last decade – although peanut allergy, the best known of the fatal allergies, is not a nut allergy at all as peanuts are not nuts but legumes like lentils or peas.

Nut allergy/intolerance is usually serious. It causes the throat to swell up so that the sufferer cannot breathe and dramatically reduces blood pressure. If you suspect you have a nut allergy you should consult a doctor immediately. If your allergy is thought to be serious you must carry an antidote (adrenaline) at all times since even the tiniest amount of allergen could set off a reaction. (See resources section for helpful support groups.)

Sugar

Although an intolerance to sugar is rare, many people experience problems with it as a result of diabetes (when the body manufactures too little or too much insulin to allow it to cope satisfactorily with sugar) or candida, a yeast infection fed by sugar. Sugar is contained naturally in many foods but it is usually the processed forms that cause problems. Whole fruit or fruit concentrates are often more acceptable to diabetics because they are absorbed more slowly into the blood stream than processed sugar.

What to do if You Suspect You Have a Food Intolerance

Whatever medical problem you have, it is always wise to make your doctor your first port of call. He or she may immediately suspect a food intolerance and suggest some dietary management, but as food intolerance is still a relatively new and untried area of medical expertise, it is possible that your doctor may not be fully aware of it. Your next move should be to start keeping a 'food diary' in which you conscientiously note everything you eat or drink and your state of health before and after. This may be a bore but after three or four weeks a pattern should start to emerge. Note also whether you have a craving for any particular food, as that is often an indication that your body may have a problem coping with it. This will be very useful information to present to your doctor or any other medical practitioner when you see them.

It is very important that you do not undertake any dietary manipulation except under medical supervision.

This is especially vital for children, older people or for anyone who is on medication or suffers from some other illness. Dramatically reducing your intake of a certain type of food may in some cases cause both deficiency and serious imbalance in the system, leading to a far more serious condition than that caused by the food intolerance.

If your food diary indicates that your problems could be related to your diet you should seek further help. If a return visit to your GP achieves little more than before you could ask to be referred to your local hospital or community dietician, or to a dietary specialist.

You could also ask to be referred – or refer yourself – to a complementary practitioner. Diet features heavily in most complementary and alternative therapies both as a diagnostic technique and as a form of treatment; it is part of their holistic (or whole body) approach to medicine. Nutritional therapists, naturopaths, herbalists, homeopaths, acupuncturists, aromatherapists and many more will include food intolerance in their assessment of your case. However, before consulting a complementary practitioner do be sure to check their credentials with the relevant professional organization. They should have had several years (not weeks) training and carry practitioner insurance.

Under expert guidance the usual course is to put you on an 'elimination diet' during which you exclude any suspect food from your diet. If your symptoms improve, the normal practice is then to 'challenge' your body by re-introducing the suspect food.

There are also now a number of 'allergy tests' available. Their accuracy varies from around 60–85% but they can be helpful to put you on the right track. Many also provide you with excellent back up material, which can be very helpful in understanding the whole business of food intolerance. However, some of these tests are quite expensive and you should be wary if they diagnose too wide a range of allergic foods. Consult your doctor or a dietician before going on too drastic an exclusion diet.

However, all this 'diagnosing' can take several months – and, in the meantime, you need to be able to feed yourself!

Coping with Food Intolerance

The first thing to realise is that having to give up all dairy products or any food containing wheat or gluten may not be as disastrous as you think. There are still lots of delicious dishes that you will be able to eat – indeed you may find some ways of eating that you actually prefer. Certainly when my family had to give up milk we found that a bowl of muesli with fresh apple or cranberry juice tastes infinitely nicer than the same bowl of muesli with milk!

However, you should also realize that from now on you must take responsibility for your diet. No more just accepting what people give you. You must scrutinize labels and familiarize yourself with the more obscure terminology of your intolerance. There has been more than one tragic case where a seriously allergic person misread a label (not knowing, for example, that casein and whey are both derived from milk) with fatal consequences. This is only likely to be a risk for someone suffering from a severe allergy rather than an intolerance but nevertheless it pays to be careful.

Here is a list of the foods that you should avoid. (N.B. CI means check ingredients.)

Soya

Lecithin	Vegetable protein and hydro-
Vegetable fat (CI)	lysed / textured vegetable
Vegetable oil (CI)	protein
	Soya Sauce

Sugar

Corn syrup	Honey
Dextrose	Invert syrup
Fructose	Maltose
Fruit juices (CI)	Malt syrup
Fruit sugar	Maple syrup
Glucose	Molasses
Glucose syrup	Sucrose
Golden syrup	Treacle

Gluten

Barley

Beer

Bran

Cereal filler

Cheese spread & dips (Cl)

Fruit drinks (Cl)

Malt

Margarine (Cl)

Modified starch

Oats

Rusk

Rye

Salad dressing (Cl)

Sauces (Cl)

Sausages (Cl)

Semolina

Starch

Sweets (Cl)

Tinned meat containing
  preservatives (Cl)

Tinned vegetables (Cl)

Wheat flour

Yeast and Fermented Foods

Alcoholic drinks

Biscuits/crackers (Cl)

Breads (Cl)

Cakes (Cl)

Cheese

Monosodium Glutamate (Cl)

Nutritional supplements (Cl)

Soya sauce

Stuffing mixes / coatings (Cl)

Vinegar

Eggs

Albumen

Conalbumin

Egg white

Egg yolk

Ovalbumin

Ovomucoid

Ovoglobulin

Vitellin

Vitellenin

Dairy

Animal fat (CI)
Artificial cream
Batter (may contain milk)
Butter
Buttermilk
Casein
Caseinates (paracaseinates)
Cheese including cream, curd & cottage cheese
Chocolate (CI)
Cream, double, whipping and single
Crème fraiche
Ghee
Hydrolysed casein/whey
Lactose
Low fat etc spreads – (CI carefully)
Milk solids
Non milk fat solids
Skimmed milk powder
Vegetable fat (CI)
Whey
Whey protein/sugar
Yoghurt

Wheat

Cereal filler
Couscous
Curry powder
Farina
Horseradish creams (CI)
Instant hot drinks including coffee, tea, chocolate (CI)
Ketchup (CI)
Modified starch
Monosodium Glutamate
Mustards (CI)
Prepared meats (CI)
Rusk
Salad dressing (CI)
Sauces (CI)
Sausages (CI)
Seasoning mixes (CI)
Semolina
Soups (CI)
Soy sauce (except wheat-free tamari) and most other Chinese sauces (CI)
Sweets (candy) (CI)
White pepper in restaurants (can be adulterated with flour)

Healthfood shops normally stock a good selection of books on food intolerance which will give you more information on your particular problem, while many large manufacturers and retailers can now provide you with lists of their products which do not contain your forbidden foods.

You will need to spend a good deal more time in the kitchen as it is difficult to find ready made products which do not contain at least one of your forbidden foods. This could, however, be an excellent thing as you will no doubt find yourself eating a far healthier diet as a result – which should in turn, help your body to re-establish its own balance and, in due course, eliminate your intolerance.

Many people who discover they have a food intolerance worry that they will no longer be able to eat out in restaurants or with friends. This need not be the case.

Phone the restaurant in advance to check that they will be able to provide you with something that you can eat. Once you arrive, explain politely, but firmly, to the waiter that you have a *serious* allergy to a specific food. There was a time when chefs would ignore requests for butter free vegetables and the like on the grounds that the customers were being 'faddy', but things have improved. However, you must insist that your message gets passed to the kitchen. A successful way of ensuring this is to tell the waiter that if you eat any of the 'banned' food you will be instantly and violently sick. He or she may not believe you but no 'wait-person' wishes to risk one of their customers throwing up all over the restaurant!

As for eating out with friends, give them plenty of warning. If they are competent cooks, provided they know exactly what it is that you cannot eat, they may be perfectly happy to make a special dish for you – or make a dish for the whole party that you can eat. Should you have any doubts about their ability to cope, I suggest that you bring your own food with you. If they get upset about this you can always tell them that your doctor has told you to take your own food when you go out.

Finding Suitable Foods

Since mandatory labelling of foods was introduced the food intolerant's life has become a great deal easier. However, labelling is still not sufficiently detailed, especially if you suffer from a serious, anaphylactic (whole body) allergy. A substance that forms only a tiny proportion of a product may not need to be declared on the label, yet a tiny amount of peanut would be sufficient to kill someone with a severe allergy. So, if you do have a serious problem, reading the label and understanding the terminology may not be enough; you will need to find a product that specifically states that it is free of the substances that you have to avoid.

Labelling can also be very confusing. Take sugar, for example. Regulations state that a product can be described as sugar free if it contains no sucrose. However, there are many forms of processed sugar and a 'sugar free' food could be high in one or several of the substances listed on page xiii.

It is particularly important for coeliacs and wheat intolerants to understand the product information on labels because gluten and wheat starch are used in so many manufactured products and cooking ingredients – such as baking powder or curry powder. However, coeliacs are fortunate in that the Coeliac Society (see page 121) produces a very comprehensive booklet listing a wide range of gluten free manufactured products.

Finding such products is not as hard as it once was. Supermarkets are beginning to stock more special diet foods and most have customer information services which will be able to point you in the right direction. (This is the case in the UK – supermarkets are not so helpful in the US or in Europe.) A good shop will normally carry plenty of special diet products and an increasing number of such products are now sold by mail order.

Many shops now also stock a certain number of organic foods, both fresh and preserved. If you are trying to rebuild your general health and immunities, it would be as well to eat as much organic food as possible. Although studies of the effects of pesticides residues are, as yet, inconclusive, it is generally believed that the fewer chemicals in the food you eat the less harm – and the more good – it is likely to do you.

How to Use this Book

The recipes in this book have been designed to inspire you to experiment within your new cookery guidelines. Do not feel that you have to stick rigidly to every ingredient or every quantity – some people think ginger is wonderful and would eat lots of it, while others enjoy only a slight flavour but no more.

The recipes aim to cater for as wide a range of intolerances as possible, hence the notes at the beginning of each one are quite complex. Please read them before you embark on the recipe.

Nutritional Information

Where a recipe says that it is dairy free, gluten free, wheat free or egg free that means that it has none of those ingredients in it. Where a recipe says that it is dairy, gluten, wheat or egg free if a particular ingredient is omitted, there will usually be two alternative ingredients of which one is dairy free, for example, for those who cannot tolerate dairy products while the other includes dairy products for those who can.

If a recipe says that it has no added sugar this means that it has no extra sugar, only sugars already present naturally in the ingredients. Some recipes contain fructose; these are not marked as no added sugar, although they may be acceptable in small quantities for anyone trying to avoid sugar.

The table accompanying each recipe gives a breakdown of its nutritional content and specifies whether this is per portion or per recipe. It lists the number of kilo calories and kilo Joules; the protein content; the total amount of fat, including a breakdown into saturated fat, monounsaturated fatty acids (MUFA) and polyunsaturated fatty acids (PUFA); the carbohydrate content, including the percentage of carbohydrate that is sugar; and the fibre content. The nutritional breakdown should be taken as a guide only. Inevitably, one person's idea of a medium-sized carrot will be different from another's, so it is impossible to guarantee that every measurement is entirely accurate. However, the figures will give you a very good idea of the nutritional content of each dish. You should be aware that the figures for fat (saturated, monounsaturated and polyunsaturated) do not always add up exactly to the total fat content. This is because there are other fats which go to make up the total fat content but in such tiny quantities that they are not measurable for the purposes of this book.

Soups and Starters

Soups and starters are easy to deal with if you have a food intolerance, as most are relatively simple and straightforward in terms of ingredients – which means that everyone else at the table can eat a totally non-allergenic starter and not even be aware of it!

Vegetable Stock

(nutritional content – negligible)

DAIRY, GLUTEN, WHEAT AND EGG FREE; NO ADDED SUGAR

MAKES ABOUT
1 LITRE
(1¾ PINTS/
4 CUPS)

PREPARATION
AND COOKING
TIME: 2½
HOURS

1 tablespoon olive or sunflower oil
1 onion, chopped roughly
1 carrot, sliced
3 mushrooms, chopped roughly
2 sprigs of fresh parsley
2 bay leaves
2 sprigs of fresh thyme or 1 teaspoon dried
8 black peppercorns
½ teaspoon sea salt
1.5 litres (2½ pints/6¼ cups) water

Optional Extras:
1 parsnip, swede, turnip or other root vegetable,
chopped roughly
1 leek or 2 shallots, chopped roughly
4 Brussels sprouts or 1 cabbage leaf
a handful of fresh spinach, chopped roughly

Heat the oil in a large saucepan and gently
cook the onion, carrot and mushrooms, plus
any of the optional extras you are using, for
10–15 minutes or until they have softened
and are beginning to brown slightly.
Add the herbs, peppercorns, salt and water,
bring to the boil, then reduce the heat and
simmer gently for at least 2 hours. Leave to
cool and then strain.

Chicken Stock

(nutritional content – negligible)

DAIRY, GLUTEN, WHEAT AND EGG FREE; NO ADDED SUGAR

**MAKES ABOUT
I LITRE
(1¾ PINTS/
4 CUPS)**

**PREPARATION
AND COOKING
TIME: 2½
HOURS**

I chicken carcass or 2 chicken joints
I onion, chopped roughly
I carrot, sliced
3 mushrooms, chopped roughly
2 sprigs of fresh parsley
2 bay leaves
2 sprigs of fresh thyme or I teaspoon dried
8 black peppercorns
½ teaspoon sea salt
1.5 litre (2½ pints/6¼ cups) water
150 ml (¼ pint/⅔ cup) dry white wine (*optional*)

Put the chicken in a large saucepan with the
vegetables, herbs, peppercorns, salt, water and
the wine, if used.
Bring to the boil, skim off any scum that rises
to the surface, then reduce the heat and
simmer gently for at least two hours.
Leave to cool and then strain.

Curried Parsnip and Apple Soup

DAIRY, GLUTEN, WHEAT AND EGG FREE; NO ADDED SUGAR

SERVES FOUR

PREPARATION
AND COOKING
TIME:
45 MINUTES

2 tablespoons vegetable oil

½ tablespoon gluten and wheat-free curry powder

175g (6 oz/1½ cups) leeks, sliced

300g (10 oz/2 cups) parsnips, sliced thinly

175g (6 oz/1½ cups) cooking apples, peeled, cored and chopped

1 litre (1¾ pints/4 cups) chicken or vegetable stock (bouillon) (see *pages 2–3*)

100 ml (3½ fl oz/⅓ cup) soya milk

100 ml (3½ fl oz/⅓ cup) dry white wine

2 tart eating apples, peeled, cored and chopped finely

sea salt and freshly ground black pepper

PER PORTION	
Kcal	200
Kjoules	820
Protein	4g
Tot. fat	9g
Sat. fat	1g
MUFA	3g
PUFA	4g
Carb.	21g
of which tot. sugar	15g
Fibre	6g

Heat the oil in a heavy-based saucepan and stir in the curry powder.

Add the leeks, parsnips and cooking apple and cook over a low heat for 10–15 minutes or until the leeks are quite soft and the parsnips are beginning to soften.

Add the stock (bouillon), soya milk and wine, bring to the boil and simmer for 30–35 minutes, until the parsnips are cooked.

Purée in a food processor or liquidiser, then pour the soup back into the pan, reheat and adjust the seasoning to taste. Just before serving, stir in the chopped eating apples.

Clear Onion and Mushroom Soup

SERVES FOUR

PREPARATION AND COOKING TIME: I HOUR

2 tablespoons olive or vegetable oil
250g (8 oz/2 cups) onions, sliced finely
250g (8 oz/2 cups) large flat mushrooms, chopped finely
300 ml (½ pint/1⅓ cups) dry white wine
900 ml (1½ pints/3¾ cups) water
sea salt and freshly ground black pepper
chopped chives, to garnish

Heat the oil in a heavy saucepan, add the onions and mushrooms and cook very slowly until they are both quite soft.
Add the wine and water, bring to the boil, then season lightly and simmer for 30–35 minutes.
Adjust the seasoning to taste, garnish with chopped chives and then serve.

PER PORTION	
Kcal	150
Kjoules	610
Protein	2g
Tot. fat	8g
Sat. fat	1g
MUFA	5g
PUFA	1g
Carb.	6g
of which tot. sugar	4g
Fibre	2g

Cauliflower and Horseradish Soup

DAIRY, GLUTEN, WHEAT AND EGG FREE; NO ADDED SUGAR

SERVES FOUR

PREPARATION
AND COOKING
TIME:
45 MINUTES

1 onion, chopped
375g (12 oz/3 cups) cauliflower, chopped
1 litre (1¾ pints/4 cups) water
2 heaped tablespoons horseradish sauce (*check ingredients label*)
4 tablespoons chopped fresh parsley (*optional*)
sea salt and freshly ground black pepper

Put the onion and cauliflower in a pan with water, bring to the boil and simmer for 30 minutes.
Purée in a food processor or liquidiser and then return the soup to the pan.
Put the horseradish in a small bowl and mix it to a smooth paste with a little of the soup. Add it to the soup with seasoning to taste – you will need quite a lot.
Stir in the chopped parsley, if used, just before serving.

PER PORTION	
Kcal	50
Kjoules	200
Protein	4g
Tot. fat	1g
Sat. fat	-
MUFA	-
PUFA	-
Carb.	6g
of which tot. sugar	5g
Fibre	2g

Gazpacho

SERVES SIX

PREPARATION
AND COOKING
TIME:
1½ HOURS

625g (1¼ lb/3 cups) ripe tomatoes, chopped
roughly
2 large garlic cloves, crushed
1 small onion, chopped finely
4 tablespoons olive oil
200 ml (7 fl oz/¾ cup) dry white wine
400 ml (14 fl oz/½ cup) chicken or vegetable stock
(bouillon) (see pages 2–3)
juice of 1 lemon
40g (1½ oz/⅓ cup) each celery, red pepper and
cucumber, chopped finely
sea salt and freshly ground black pepper

PER PORTION	
Kcal	140
Kjoules	575
Protein	1g
Tot. fat	11g
Sat. fat	2g
MUFA	7g
PUFA	1g
Carb.	5g
of which tot. sugar	5g
Fibre	2g

Put the tomatoes in a large pan with the
garlic, onion, oil, wine and stock (bouillon).
Bring to the boil and simmer for 1 hour.
Purée the soup in a food processor or
liquidiser, then pass it through a sieve to
remove the tomato pips.
Add the lemon juice and salt and pepper
to taste. Chill the soup.
Just before serving, check the seasoning again
and stir in the chopped vegetables. Garnish
with a little coarsely ground black pepper.

Fennel and Haddock Soup

DAIRY, GLUTEN, WHEAT AND EGG FREE; NO ADDED SUGAR

SERVES FOUR

PREPARATION AND COOKING TIME: 45 MINUTES

2 tablespoons olive or vegetable oil
1 small bulb of fennel, sliced finely
2 large spring onions (scallions), sliced finely
2 large anchovy fillets, chopped finely
75g (3 oz/1 cup) mushrooms, sliced
900 ml (1½ pints/3¾ cups) water
200 ml (7 fl oz/¾ cup) dry white wine
250g (8 oz/1½ cups) haddock fillets, diced
50g (2 oz/½ cup) tofu, diced finely (optional)
juice of ½ lemon
sea salt and freshly ground black pepper

Heat the oil in a pan and gently cook the fennel, spring onions (scallions) and anchovies until softened but not coloured. Add the mushrooms and continue to cook for a few minutes, then pour in the water and wine and bring slowly to the boil. Add the haddock, bring back to the boil and simmer for 5 minutes.
Stir in the tofu, if used, along with the lemon juice and seasoning. Cook for 1–2 minutes more, then remove from the heat and, if possible, set aside for about 2 hours for the flavours to mature. Reheat gently before serving.

PER PORTION	
Kcal	160
Kjoules	660
Protein	9g
Tot. fat	10g
Sat. fat	1g
MUFA	5g
PUFA	1g
Carb.	2g
of which tot. sugar	2g
Fibre	1g

Aubergine (Eggplant) Pâté

DAIRY, GLUTEN, WHEAT AND EGG FREE; NO ADDED SUGAR

SERVES
FOUR–SIX

PREPARATION
AND COOKING
TIME:
30 MINUTES

1 aubergine (eggplant) (300g/10 oz/2 cups), sliced
1–2 garlic cloves, crushed
100g (3½ oz/½ cup) cooked aduki beans
50 g (2 oz/⅔ cup) mushrooms, chopped
1 tablespoon olive oil
juice of ½–1 lemon
gluten and wheat free soy sauce
50g (2 oz/1 cup) fresh spinach leaves
2 large sprigs of fresh mint
sea salt and freshly ground black pepper

PER PORTION	
Kcal	80
Kjoules	340
Protein	4g
Tot. fat	4g
Sat. fat	1g
MUFA	2g
PUFA	1g
Carb.	8g
of which tot. sugar	2g
Fibre	3g

Steam the aubergine (eggplant) until soft and then purée in a food processor with the garlic, adzuki beans, mushrooms, oil and lemon juice. Add soy sauce and seasoning to taste, with more lemon juice if necessary. Add the spinach and mint and process briefly so that they are finely chopped but not puréed. Adjust the seasoning and serve accompanied by wholemeal toast, if you can eat it, or rice crackers. Alternatively spoon the mixture into a mould, chill, then turn it out on to a dish and serve with salad and brown bread, if you can eat it.

Avocado and Chicory Salad

SERVES FOUR

**PREPARATION TIME:
5 MINUTES**

juice of 1 large orange
1 large ripe avocado, peeled, stoned (pitted) and diced
2 small heads of chicory, shredded
fresh coriander (cilantro) or chervil, to garnish

For the French Dressing:
3 tablespoons olive or sunflower oil
juice of ½ lemon, or to taste
sea salt and freshly ground black pepper

First make the French dressing. Whisk together all the ingredients in a small bowl. Mix together the French dressing and orange juice and toss the avocado and chicory in this mixture. Transfer to a serving dish and sprinkle liberally with the coriander (cilantro) or chervil.

PER PORTION	
Kcal	200
Kjoules	810
Protein	1g
Tot. fat	20g
Sat. fat	3g
MUFA	13g
PUFA	2g
Carb.	4g
of which tot. sugar	3g
Fibre	1g

Mushrooms Stuffed with Smoked Mussels

SERVES FOUR

PREPARATION
AND COOKING
TIME:
15 MINUTES

4 large flat mushrooms
3 tablespoons olive oil
105g can smoked mussels
50g (2 oz/⅔ cup) shiitake mushrooms, chopped roughly
50g (2 oz/⅔ cup) oyster mushrooms, chopped roughly
50g (2 oz/⅔ cup) fresh, frozen or canned cockles
juice of 1 lemon
a handful of fresh parsley, chopped roughly
sea salt and freshly ground black pepper

Preheat the grill (broiler). Remove the stalks from the flat mushrooms, then drizzle ½ tablespoon of oil into each mushroom cap and grill (broil) them for 4–5 minutes, until tender.

Meanwhile, drain the oil from the smoked mussels into a pan. Add the remaining olive oil and the shiitake and oyster mushrooms. Cook briskly for 2–3 minutes, then stir in the mussels and the cockles, thawed if frozen. Cook for 2 minutes before adding the lemon juice and salt and pepper to taste.

Stir in the parsley and pile the mixture into the grilled (broiled) mushrooms. Serve at once.

PER PORTION	
Kcal	150
Kjoules	610
Protein	8g
Tot. fat	12g
Sat. fat	2g
MUFA	8g
PUFA	2g
Carb.	2g
of which tot. sugar	neg
Fibre	1g

Marinated Fried Tofu

SERVES FOUR

PREPARATION AND COOKING TIME:

30 MINUTES + MARINATING

1 teaspoon coriander seeds
25g (1 oz/⅓ cup) fresh ginger root, peeled and grated
2 large garlic cloves, crushed
1 dried chilli, chopped
juice of 1 orange
1 generous teaspoon gluten and wheat-free soy sauce (check the label for sugar)
4 tablespoons olive oil
250g (8 oz/2 cups) fairly firm tofu, cut into bite-sized pieces
1 tablespoon soya (canola) oil
2 sprigs of fresh coriander (cilantro) (for garnish)

PER PORTION	
Kcal	230
Kjoules	950
Protein	6g
Tot. fat	22g
Sat. fat	3g
MUFA	12g
PUFA	5g
Carb.	4g
of which tot. sugar	3g
Fibre	neg

Bruise the coriander seeds in a pestle and mortar or in a small bowl with the end of a rolling pin. Mix them with the ginger, garlic, chilli, orange juice, soy sauce and olive oil to make a marinade.

Put the tofu in a bowl, pour over the marinade and leave for at least 2 hours and up to 24 hours. Remove the tofu from the marinade with a slotted spoon and drain it slightly.

Heat the soya (canola) oil in a frying pan and fry the tofu gently until it is golden brown and slightly crisp on all sides. Transfer it to a serving dish and pour over the marinade.

You can serve the tofu either on cocktail sticks or with fresh brown bread, if you can eat it, or a brown rice salad.

Avocado and Strawberry Salad

SERVES FOUR

PREPARATION TIME:

5 MINUTES

2 ripe avocados
12 strawberries, quartered
juice of 1 lemon

Halve and stone (pit) the avocados, then cut out the flesh without damaging the skins. Set the skins aside and chop the avocado flesh roughly.

Gently mix the avocado and strawberries in a bowl and add the lemon juice. Turn them to coat them thoroughly with the juice, then pile the mixture into the avocado shells and serve as soon as possible.

PER PORTION	
Kcal	160
Kjoules	670
Protein	2g
Tot. fat	16g
Sat. fat	3g
MUFA	10g
PUFA	2g
Carb.	4g
of which tot. sugar	3g
Fibre	1g

Chicken Liver and Tomato Pâté

DAIRY, GLUTEN, WHEAT AND EGG FREE; NO ADDED SUGAR

SERVES FOUR

PREPARATION
AND COOKING
TIME:
30 MINUTES

2 tablespoons olive or vegetable oil
4 rashers of streaky bacon, chopped finely
3 garlic cloves, crushed
2 onions, chopped finely
375g (12 oz/1½ cups) chicken livers
2 heaped tablespoons tomato purée (paste)
6 tablespoons whisky (optional)
sea salt and freshly ground black pepper
chervil, to garnish

Heat the oil in a large frying pan and gently fry the bacon, garlic and onion until the onion is soft but not browned.

Add the chicken livers and cook for 2–3 minutes only – the livers should be just pink in the middle. Remove from the heat, add the tomato purée (paste) and then process in a liquidiser or food processor.

Add the whisky, if used, and season to taste with salt and pepper.

Spoon the pâté into four ramekin dishes or one large dish, garnish with chervil and serve with plenty of hot brown toast, if you can eat it, or rice cakes.

PER PORTION	
Kcal	320
Kjoules	1340
Protein	24g
Tot. fat	16g
Sat. fat	4g
MUFA	8g
PUFA	2g
Carb.	8g
of which tot. sugar	6g
Fibre	neg

Guacamole

SERVES FOUR

PREPARATION TIME: 15 MINUTES

2 very ripe avocados
½ small onion, chopped very finely
1 garlic clove, crushed
2 firm tomatoes, skinned, de-seeded and chopped finely
6 black olives, chopped finely
1-2 tablespoons lemon juice
several drops of Tabasco sauce

Peel and stone (pit) the avocados and purée the flesh (if they are really ripe you should be able to do this in a bowl with a wooden spoon).

Add the onion and garlic and then fold in the chopped tomatoes and olives.

Season to taste with the lemon juice and Tabasco.

Serve the guacamole as a dip with crudités or as a pâté with hot brown toast, if you can eat it, or rice cakes. Cover the guacamole tightly if it is not to be used immediately; it will brown if exposed to the air.

PER PORTION	
Kcal	180
Kjoules	730
Protein	2g
Tot. fat	18g
Sat. fat	4g
MUFA	11g
PUFA	2g
Carb.	3g
of which tot. sugar	1g
Fibre	1g

Fish, Meat and Poultry

Roast or grilled (broiled) fish or meat with boiled or steamed vegetables, delicious though they may be, are the safe but rather monotonous diet of many people with food intolerances. As a result, a pie, casserole or pasta dish with a rich and complex sauce can seem quite exciting. So here are nearly 30 of them, with not a roast in sight – apart from the Christmas turkey!

Fish Cakes
* dairy free if tofu is used

SERVES FOUR

PREPARATION AND COOKING TIME: 45 MINUTES

125g (4 oz/⅔ cup) brown rice
500g (1 lb/3 cups) white fish fillets, such as cod, haddock or coley
2 tablespoons crème fraîche, live yoghurt or silken tofu
juice of ½ lemon *(optional)*
3 tablespoons polenta
30g packet of plain potato crisps, crushed
3-4 tablespoons olive or vegetable oil
sea salt and freshly ground black pepper

Cook the rice in boiling water until it is very soft, then drain.

Purée it in a food processor with the fish and the crème fraîche, yoghurt or tofu, then stir in the lemon juice, if used, and season generously with salt and pepper. Chill the mixture thoroughly.

Mix the polenta with the crushed crisps and spread it out on a plate.

Shape generous dessertspoonfuls of the fish mixture into cakes and coat them with the polenta and crisps.

Fry the fish cakes gently in the oil for about 5 minutes on each side, until crisp and golden, then serve at once, accompanied by green vegetables or a salad.

PER PORTION	
Kcal	140
Kjoules	600
Protein	8g
Tot. fat	6g
Sat. fat	1g
MUFA	4g
PUFA	1g
Carb.	14g
of which tot. sugar	neg
Fibre	1g

Tuna Stir-Fry

SERVES FOUR

**PREPARATION
AND COOKING
TIME:
15 MINUTES**

2 tablespoons sunflower oil
1 bulb of fennel, sliced thinly
1 red pepper, sliced thinly
4 courgettes (zucchini), cut into thin matchsticks
125g (4 oz/1¼ cups) mushrooms, sliced thinly
200g can of tuna in oil
500g (1 lb/8 cups) Chinese leaves, sliced thinly
4 tablespoons sunflower seeds
juice of 1 lemon
2 handfuls of fresh parsley, chopped
sea salt and freshly ground black pepper

PER PORTION	
Kcal	380
Kjoules	1590
Protein	25g
Tot. fat	27g
Sat. fat	3g
MUFA	5g
PUFA	16g
Carb.	12g
of which tot. sugar	6g
Fibre	2g

Heat the oil in a large, heavy-based frying pan.
Add the fennel and red pepper and fry briskly
for 2 minutes.

Add the courgettes (zucchini) and
mushrooms, then break up the tuna and add
it to the pan with its oil. Stir-fry for 1–2
minutes, then add the Chinese leaves and
sunflower seeds. Continue to stir-fry for
3–4 minutes or until the Chinese leaves are
lightly cooked but still crunchy.

Add the lemon juice, salt and pepper to taste
and then sprinkle liberally with the parsley.
Serve immediately.

Smoked Mackerel and Tofu Quiche

SERVES FOUR

PREPARATION AND COOKING TIME: I HOUR

Note:
Ham, chicken, nuts or diced cooked root vegetables can be substituted for the smoked mackerel

PER PORTION	
Kcal	390
Kjoules	1615
Protein	17g
Tot. fat	28g
Sat. fat	6g
MUFA	12g
PUFA	7g
Carb.	17g
of which tot. sugar	1g
Fibre	3g

20-cm (8-inch) pastry case (shell) made from oat pastry (see page 107) or gluten-free pastry (see page 108)
1 tablespoon olive oil
50g (2 oz/⅔ cup) mushrooms, chopped roughly
300g (10 oz/2½ cups) silken tofu
175 ml (6 fl oz/⅔ cup) soya milk, or half soya milk and half dry white wine
1 smoked mackerel fillet (about 125g/4 oz/⅔ cup), flaked roughly
50g (2 oz/1 cup) fresh spinach, chopped roughly
1 teaspoon chopped fresh thyme or ½ teaspoon dried
sea salt and freshly ground black pepper

Preheat the oven to Gas Mark 4/180°C/350°F. Line the pastry case (shell) with foil or grease-proof paper, weight it with beans or rice and bake blind (empty) for about 20 minutes. Take it out of the oven, remove the paper and beans or rice and set aside.
Meanwhile, heat the oil in a pan, add the mushrooms and fry briskly for 3 minutes. Beat the tofu with a wooden spoon until smooth, then add the soya milk, or soya milk and white wine mixed, and stir to make a fairly smooth cream. Add the mushrooms, flaked mackerel, spinach and herbs and season generously.

Pour the mixture into the pastry case (shell) and bake for 20 minutes. The filling will set but it will not rise as it would with eggs, or go brown. However, the combination of white tofu, green spinach and ochre-coloured mackerel is very pretty. Serve hot or cold.

Fish Pie with Apple

SERVES FOUR

**PREPARATION
AND COOKING
TIME:
1¼ HOURS**

1 kg (2 lb/7 cups) potatoes
a knob of dairy-free margarine
3 tablespoons olive or vegetable oil
2 large leeks, sliced thinly
1 large cooking apple, peeled, cored and sliced thinly
4 white fish fillets, such as sole, cod or haddock (about 125g/4 oz/⅔ cup each)
1 tablespoon sunflower seeds
sea salt and freshly ground black pepper
chopped fresh parsley, to garnish

Preheat the oven to Gas Mark 4/180°C/350°F.
Steam or boil the potatoes until tender. Peel them, or not if you prefer, and mash them with the margarine and salt and pepper.
Pour most of the oil into an ovenproof casserole dish and scatter the leeks over it. Cover the leeks with the sliced apple and lay the fish fillets on top. Season lightly.
Cover the fish with the mashed potato and sprinkle over the sunflower seeds. Drizzle on the remaining oil and bake for 45 minutes, or microwave in a 650/750-watt oven on full power for 15 minutes (if you cook the pie in a microwave the top will not brown).
Sprinkle with parsley and serve accompanied by a green vegetable.

PER PORTION	
Kcal	650
Kjoules	2740
Protein	34g
Tot. fat	18g
Sat. fat	3g
MUFA	9g
PUFA	5g
Carb.	93g
of which tot. sugar	8g
Fibre	11g

Barbecued Fish en Papillote

DAIRY, GLUTEN, WHEAT AND EGG FREE; NO ADDED SUGAR

SERVES FOUR

PREPARATION
AND COOKING
TIME:
30 MINUTES +
MARINATING

4 salmon, cod or haddock steaks (150g/5 oz/¾ cup each)
4 tablespoons olive or vegetable oil
3 shallots or spring onions (scallions), chopped finely
1 garlic clove, crushed
a handful of fresh parsley, chopped
2 tablespoons wine vinegar
grated zest of 1 lime or 1 small lemon
sea salt and freshly ground black pepper

PER PORTION	
Kcal	240
Kjoules	980
Protein	21g
Tot. fat	16g
Sat. fat	2g
MUFA	11g
PUFA	2g
Carb.	2g
of which tot. sugar	2g
Fibre	1g

Put the fish in a shallow saucepan or a microwave-proof dish, pour over boiling water to cover and simmer for 5 minutes, or microwave in a 650/750-watt oven on full power for 2 minutes. Drain the fish carefully. Mix together all the remaining ingredients to make a marinade and pour it into a glass or porcelain dish that is large enough to hold the fish in a single layer. Put the fish steaks in the dish and spoon the marinade over them. Cover and leave for 6–12 hours.

Prepare a barbecue or preheat the grill (broiler). Put each fish steak and some of the marinade on a large square of well-oiled greaseproof paper, fold it in half to enclose the fish completely and then fold the edges together to seal. Cook the fish parcels on a barbecue or under a hot grill (broiler) for about 6–8 minutes, depending on the thickness of the fish.

Pasta and Fresh Salmon & Spinach

*gluten and egg free, depending on pasta used

DAIRY AND WHEAT FREE; NO ADDED SUGAR

SERVES FOUR
AS A MAIN
COURSE, SIX
AS A STARTER

PREPARATION
AND COOKING
TIME:
30 MINUTES

6-8 tablespoons good quality olive oil

1 onion, chopped finely

175g (6 oz/1⅓ cups) young courgettes (zucchini), cut into thin matchsticks

375g (12 oz/6 cups) fresh spinach, chopped roughly

375g (12 oz/2 cups) cooked fresh salmon, flaked finely

juice of 1–2 lemons

375g (12 oz/4 cups) fresh tagliatelle, gluten and wheat-free pasta or egg-free rice noodles

sea salt and freshly ground black pepper

First cook the pasta in plenty of fast-boiling water until just tender.

Meanwhile, heat the oil in a heavy pan and gently fry the onion until softened.

Add the courgettes (zucchini) and continue to cook for 1–2 minutes, then stir in the spinach. Cover and cook for a few minutes or until the spinach is wilted, then add the salmon and lemon juice to taste. Season with salt and pepper.

Drain and toss the pasta thoroughly with the salmon and spinach mixture. Adjust the seasoning to taste and serve at once.

PER PORTION	
Kcal	470
Kjoules	1930
Protein	23g
Tot. fat	39g
Sat. fat	6g
MUFA	24g
PUFA	7g
Carb.	5g
of which tot. sugar	4g
Fibre	4g

Pasta with Tomato and Ham Sauce

*gluten and egg free, depending on pasta used

SERVES FOUR

PREPARATION AND COOKING TIME: 45 MINUTES

3 tablespoons olive or vegetable oil
2 onions, chopped finely
4 celery sticks, chopped very finely
125g (4 oz/1⅓ cups) mushrooms, sliced thinly
397g (14 oz/1¾ cups) can chopped tomatoes
150 ml (¼ pint/⅔ cup) dry white wine or
vegetable stock (bouillon) (see *page 2*)
2 teaspoons dried marjoram
50g (2 oz/¼ cup) cooked ham, chopped
500g (1 lb/2½ cups) noodles, gluten and wheat-
free pasta or egg-free rice noodles
sea salt and freshly ground black pepper

Heat the oil in a heavy pan and gently cook
the onions and celery until soft.
Add the mushrooms and continue to cook for
a few minutes.
Add the tomatoes, wine or stock (bouillon),
marjoram and a little seasoning. Bring to the
boil and simmer gently for 20–30 minutes.
Adjust the seasoning to taste and stir in the
chopped ham.
Meanwhile, cook the noodles in plenty of
fast-boiling water until just tender. Drain
quickly and transfer them to a dish. Spoon
over the sauce and serve at once.

PER PORTION	
Kcal	630
Kjoules	2640
Protein	18g
Tot. fat	19g
Sat. fat	3g
MUFA	10g
PUFA	5g
Carb.	95g
of which tot. sugar	8g
Fibre	10g

Duck with Apple and Orange Sauce

DAIRY, GLUTEN, WHEAT AND EGG FREE; NO ADDED SUGAR

SERVES FOUR

PREPARATION AND COOKING TIME: 2 HOURS

1.25–1.75 kg (3–4 lb/6–8 cups) duck
2 bay leaves
1 kg (2 lb/8½ cups) leeks, sliced quite thickly
1 large cooking apple, peeled, cored and sliced
juice of 2 large oranges
150 ml (¼ pint/⅔ cup) white wine or water
sea salt and freshly ground black pepper

Preheat the oven to Gas Mark 5/190°C/375°F. Prick the duck all over with a fork; put the bay leaves in the body cavity. Put the duck on a rack in a roasting tin and roast for 30 minutes, then remove from the oven. Reduce the heat to Gas Mark 4/180°C/350°F.

Put the leeks in a casserole and cover with the sliced apple. Place the duck on top.

Pour over the orange juice and wine or water. Season well, cover and cook for 1 hour, until the duck is tender.

PER PORTION	
Kcal	300
Kjoules	1260
Protein	30g
Tot. fat	11g
Sat. fat	3g
MUFA	5g
PUFA	2g
Carb.	15g
of which tot. sugar	14g
Fibre	8g

Turkey or Chicken Risotto

DAIRY, GLUTEN, WHEAT AND EGG FREE; NO ADDED SUGAR

SERVES FOUR

PREPARATION
AND COOKING
TIME:
45 MINUTES

2 tablespoons vegetable oil
1 leek, chopped roughly
50g (2 oz/⅔ cup) mushrooms, halved or quartered
250g (8 oz/1¼ cups) brown rice
350 ml (12 fl oz/1½ cups) water or chicken stock
(bouillon) (see page 2)
75g (3 oz/1 cup) fresh or frozen French beans,
sliced finely, or peas
1 tablespoon raisins (optional)
175g (6 oz/¾ cup) cooked turkey or chicken,
pulled or cut in small pieces
sea salt and freshly ground black pepper

PER PORTION	
Kcal	367
Kjoules	1525
Protein	17g
Tot. fat	10.5g
Sat. fat	2g
MUFA	3g
PUFA	4g
Carb.	52g
of which tot. sugar	1.2g
Fibre	2.5g

Heat the oil in a saucepan, add the leek and
fry gently until it is just beginning to soften.
Add the mushrooms and cook for 2 minutes.
Add the rice, stir for 1–2 minutes, then add
the water or stock (bouillon). Stir well, then
bring to the boil and simmer, uncovered, for
15–20 minutes or until the rice is cooked and
all the liquid has been absorbed. (If the liquid
is absorbed before the rice is done, add a little
more.)

If you are using fresh beans or peas, blanch
them briefly in boiling water. Add the beans
or peas to the risotto along with the raisins, if
used. Stir in the turkey or chicken and cook
for a few minutes to heat through, then season
to taste and serve.

This risotto is good either hot or cold.

Chicken Salad

SERVES FOUR

PREPARATION TIME: 15 MINUTES

500g (1 lb/2 cups) cooked chicken, diced
grated zest and juice of 2 lemons
1 tart eating apple, diced
1 small onion, chopped very finely
2 handfuls of fresh parsley, chopped
2–3 tablespoons olive oil
sea salt and freshly ground black pepper
mixed salad leaves, to serve

Mix together the chicken, lemon zest, apple, onion and parsley.
Sprinkle with salt and pepper then add the lemon juice and olive oil.
Mix well together and serve on a bed of mixed salad leaves.

PER PORTION	
Kcal	250
Kjoules	1050
Protein	25g
Tot. fat	15g
Sat. fat	3g
MUFA	9g
PUFA	2g
Carb.	5g
of which tot. sugar	4g
Fibre	1g

Top: Curried Parsnip and
Apple Soup, page 4
Below: Clear Onion
and Mushroom
Soup, page 5

Avocado and Chicory
Salad, page 10

Mushrooms
stuffed with Smoked
Mussels, page 11

Fish Pie
with Apple,
page 22

Barbecued Fish
en Papillote, page 23

Turkey or Chicken
Risotto, page 27

Chicken Salad,
page 28

Roast Turkey, page 32
Chestnut Stuffing, page 33

Quinoa and Cashew
Stuffing, page 35

Rice 'Bread Sauce',
page 36

Moussaka, page 37

Braised Lamb
with Vegetables,
page 40

Pasta Primavera,
page 43

Penne Paesana, page 48

Top: Potato and Polenta Bake with Apple Sauce, page 52

Below: Mushroom and Nut Risotto, page 55

Bacon and Cabbage Casserole

SERVES FOUR

PREPARATION
AND COOKING
TIME:
1 HOUR

250g (8 oz/1⅓ cups) back bacon, chopped quite finely

1 large onion, chopped finely

4 tablespoons olive or vegetable oil

12 juniper berries

500g (1 lb/8 cups) green or Savoy cabbage, sliced quite thinly

1 large cooking apple, peeled, cored and chopped

200 ml (7 fl oz/¾ cup) red wine or vegetable stock (bouillon) (see page 2)

125g (4 oz/1⅓ cups) large flat mushrooms, sliced

sea salt and freshly ground black pepper

Put the bacon and onion in a large pan with 1 tablespoon of the oil and fry them until the bacon has started to crisp and the onion to brown.

Bruise the juniper berries in a pestle and mortar or with the end of a rolling pin and add them to the pan with the cabbage, apple and red wine or vegetable stock (bouillon). Cover and cook gently for 15 minutes.

In a separate pan, cook the mushrooms briskly in the remaining oil, then add them to the cabbage mixture. Continue to cook, covered, for 15 minutes. The cabbage should be just cooked but still slightly crisp. Season to taste and serve as a main dish or as an accompaniment to roast meat.

PER PORTION	
Kcal	350
Kjoules	1450
Protein	17g
Tot. fat	21g
Sat. fat	4g
MUFA	12g
PUFA	3g
Carb.	17g
of which tot. sugar	15g
Fibre	7g

Beef or Veal à la Mode

SERVES FOUR

**PREPARATION
AND COOKING
TIME:
4 HOURS**

1 kg (2 lb) blade of beef or breast of veal, boned, trimmed and cut into large pieces

about 3 level tablespoons cornflour (cornstarch) seasoned with salt and pepper

3 tablespoons olive or vegetable oil

2 large onions, chopped finely

750 ml (1¼ pints/3 cups) boiling water

3 large bay leaves, crushed lightly

8 allspice berries, crushed lightly

Toss the meat in the seasoned cornflour (cornstarch), making sure it is well coated. Heat the oil in a heavy pan, then add the onions and the meat and fry briskly for about 8 minutes, until the meat is well browned all over.

Add any leftover cornflour (cornstarch) and continue to cook for a few minutes, then add the boiling water and stir well to scrape up the sediment from the bottom of the pan.

Add the bay leaves and allspice, cover the pan and reduce the heat to very low or transfer everything to a slow cooker. Cook at just below a simmer for 3–3½ hours (6–8 hours in a slow cooker).

Leave to cool completely and then remove any excess fat from the top.

To serve, reheat the beef and adjust the seasoning. Serve with baked potatoes and a green vegetable or salad.

PER PORTION	
Kcal	350
Kjoules	1470
Protein	27g
Tot. fat	17g
Sat. fat	4g
MUFA	10g
PUFA	2g
Carb.	24g
of which tot. sugar	6g
Fibre	2g

London Pie

*dairy free if butter, milk/cream and cheese are omitted

GLUTEN, WHEAT AND EGG FREE; NO ADDED SUGAR

SERVES FOUR

PREPARATION
AND COOKING
TIME:
1¼ HOURS

500g (1 lb/2 cups) minced beef or pork
2 onions, chopped finely
1 cooking apple, peeled, cored and chopped finely
2 tablespoons sultanas or raisins (*optional*)
2 tablespoons tomato purée (paste)
a generous dash of Worcestershire sauce
150 ml (¼ pint/⅔ cup) chicken stock (bouillon)
(see *page 3*)
1 kg (2 lb/7 cups) potatoes, chopped
a knob of butter or dairy-free margarine
a little milk or cream, or soya milk
50g (2 oz/¼ cup) well-flavoured cheese, grated, or
30g packet of potato crisps, crushed
sea salt and freshly ground black pepper

PER PORTION	
Kcal	540
Kjoules	2300
Protein	35g
Tot. fat	21g
Sat. fat	12g
MUFA	6g
PUFA	1g
Carb.	57g
of which tot. sugar	18g
Fibre	6g

Preheat the oven to Gas Mark 4/180°C/350°F. Put the meat in an ovenproof dish and mix in the onions, apple, and the sultanas or raisins, if used. Mix together the tomato purée (paste), Worcestershire sauce and stock (bouillon), season and pour it over the meat. Cover the dish with foil or a lid and bake for 30 minutes. Meanwhile, boil or steam the potatoes, then mash them with the butter or margarine and the milk, cream or soya milk. Season them and mix in half the cheese, if used.
When the meat is cooked, spoon the potato over it, sprinkle over the rest of the cheese or the crushed crisps and return the dish to the oven for 15 minutes or until the topping is browned. Serve at once.

Roast Turkey
*dairy free if butter is omitted

SERVES SIX

**PREPARATION
AND COOKING
TIME:
3–4 HOURS**

3.5–4.5 kg (10 lb) turkey
about 600 ml (1 pint/2½ cups) chicken stock
(bouillon) (see *page 3*) or water
1 recipe of Quinoa and Cashew Stuffing (see *page 35*) or Chestnut Stuffing (see *page 33*), or use
both stuffings, one for each end
200g (7 oz/1⅓ cups) streaky bacon rashers
a little butter or oil

Preheat the oven to Gas Mark 4/180°C/350°F.
Put a baking rack in a roasting tin and fill the tin with chicken stock (bouillon) or water to come just below the level of the rack.
Stuff the bird at both ends and tie it well.
Place it on the rack over the liquid and cover the breast with the rashers of streaky bacon and/or foil or greaseproof paper that has been well rubbed with butter or olive oil.
Roast the turkey for 20 minutes for each 500g (1 lb). Make sure the liquid does not dry up and, approximately half way through the cooking, remove the greaseproof paper or foil from the breast and reduce the oven temperature to Gas Mark 3/160°C/350°F.
Roasting the bird over the liquid keeps it much moister than it would otherwise be.
Serve with Rice 'Bread' Sauce (*see page 36*) and Gravy (*see page 34*).

PER PORTION	
Kcal	**490**
Kjoules	**2040**
Protein	**41g**
Tot. fat	**36g**
Sat. fat	**14g**
MUFA	**16g**
PUFA	**neg**
Carb.	**–**
of which tot. sugar	**–**
Fibre	**–**

Chestnut Stuffing

MAKES
ENOUGH FOR
I MEDIUM
TURKEY

PREPARATION
AND COOKING
TIME:
15 MINUTES

375g (12 oz/2 cups) unsweetened chestnut purée or canned whole chestnuts
175 ml (6 fl oz/⅔ cup) olive or vegetable oil
6 tablespoons medium sweet sherry, Marsala or port
375g (12 oz/2 cups) canned chickpeas (garbanzo beans) (*check the label for sugar*)
6 tablespoons sunflower seeds
sea salt and freshly ground black pepper

Put the chestnut purée or chestnuts in a food processor with the oil and the sherry, Marsala or port and process until it is smooth.
Add the chickpeas (garbanzo beans) and purée – just briefly if you prefer some 'crunch'.
Transfer the mixture to a bowl, stir in the sunflower seeds and season to taste.
You can use this stuffing inside the bird, bake it in little balls alongside the bird – or even serve it as a pate on toast!

PER PORTION	
Kcal	840
Kjoules	3450
Protein	12g
Tot. fat	60g
Sat. fat	9g
MUFA	36g
PUFA	15g
Carb.	54g
of which tot. sugar	9g
Fibre	6g

Gravy

**MAKES ABOUT
I LITRE (1¾
PINTS/4 CUPS)**

**PREPARATION
AND COOKING
TIME:
1½ HOURS**

giblets from the turkey
I carrot, chopped roughly
I onion, chopped roughly
I celery stick, chopped roughly
mushroom stalks, chopped roughly (*optional*)
I tomato, chopped roughly
a handful of peppercorns
I bay leaf
1.2 litres (2 pints/5 cups) vegetable stock
(bouillon) (*see page 2*) or 1.2 litres (2 pints/
5 cups) water plus a dash of wine or sherry
25g (1 oz/⅛ cup) dairy-free margarine or fat from
the turkey
40g (1½ oz/⅓ cup) arrowroot
150 ml (¼ pint/⅔ cup) Marsala, port or red wine
(*optional*)
sea salt and freshly ground black pepper

PER PORTION	
Kcal	120
Kjoules	490
Protein	neg
Tot. fat	5g
Sat. fat	2g
MUFA	2g
PUFA	Ig
Carb.	12g
of which tot. sugar	neg
Fibre	neg

Put the giblets in a pan with the vegetables,
peppercorns, bay leaf and liquid. Bring to the
boil, simmer for 1 hour and then strain. Heat
the margarine or turkey fat in a pan. Mix the
arrowroot with a little of the stock (bouillon)
to make a thick paste then add to the fat in
the pan. Heat gently, stirring continually and
gradually add more stock (bouillon) a little at
a time, until the mixture thickens. Continue
to cook for 15 minutes, then add the Marsala,
port or wine, if used, and season to taste.

Quinoa and Cashew Stuffing

DAIRY, GLUTEN, WHEAT AND EGG FREE; NO ADDED SUGAR

MAKES
ENOUGH FOR
I MEDIUM
TURKEY

PREPARATION
AND COOKING
TIME:
45 MINUTES

2 tablespoons olive or sunflower oil
I onion, chopped finely
2 garlic cloves, crushed (*optional*)
I large celery stick, chopped
100g (4 oz/I cup) quinoa
½ teaspoon dried thyme or I teaspoon fresh
300 ml (½ pint/1⅓ cups) water
150 ml (¼ pint/⅔ cup) dry white wine
75g (3 oz/½ cup) cashew nuts
a handful of fresh parsley, chopped
a dash of lemon juice
sea salt and freshly ground black pepper

Heat the oil in a pan and gently cook the
onion, garlic, if used, and celery until they are
just soft.
Add the quinoa, thyme, water and wine.
Bring to the boil and simmer gently for 15–20
minutes, adding a little more liquid if the
mixture becomes too dry. When the quinoa is
soft add the cashew nuts, parsley, lemon juice
and seasoning.

PER PORTION	
Kcal	**290**
Kjoules	**1200**
Protein	**7g**
Tot. fat	**18g**
Sat. fat	**3g**
MUFA	**9g**
PUFA	**3g**
Carb.	**22g**
of which tot. sugar	**2g**
Fibre	**2g**

Rice 'Bread' Sauce

*dairy free if soya milk used; no added sugar
if sugar/fructose is omitted

GLUTEN, WHEAT AND EGG FREE

SERVES FOUR

PREPARATION
AND COOKING
TIME:
45 MINUTES

50g (2 oz/¼ cup) white pudding rice
450 ml (¾ pint/2 cups) milk or 500 ml (18 fl oz/
2¼ cups) soya milk
1 medium onion, stuck with 6 cloves
4 peppercorns
½ teaspoon sugar or fructose (*optional*)
sea salt

Put the rice in a pan with the milk, onion and
peppercorns. Bring slowly to the boil and
simmer very gently for 20–30 minutes or until
the rice is quite soft.

Remove the cloves from the onion and purée
the milky rice in a liquidiser or food processor.
Depending on how strong an onion flavour
you like, purée the onion with the mixture or
remove it first. Season with salt, and with the
sugar or fructose, if liked.

Reheat gently before serving.

PER PORTION	
Kcal	**80**
Kjoules	**350**
Protein	**5g**
Tot. fat	**3g**
Sat. fat	**neg**
MUFA	**1g**
PUFA	**1g**
Carb.	**10g**
of which tot. sugar	**1g**
Fibre	**neg**

Moussaka

SERVES FOUR

**PREPARATION
AND COOKING
TIME:
I HOUR**

6–8 tablespoons vegetable oil
2 large aubergines (eggplants), sliced
375g (12 oz/1½ cups) cooked lamb, cubed
6 tomatoes, sliced, or 230g (7 oz/¾ cup) can chopped tomatoes
I heaped teaspoon dried marjoram
25g (1 oz/¼ cup) sunflower seeds
15g (½ oz/⅛ cup) sesame seeds
I tablespoon olive oil
200g (7 oz/1 cup) silken tofu
juice of ½–1 lemon
sea salt and freshly ground black pepper
fresh marjoram, to garnish

PER PORTION	
Kcal	570
Kjoules	2350
Protein	35g
Tot. fat	44g
Sat. fat	9g
MUFA	25g
PUFA	8g
Carb.	7g
of which tot. sugar	5g
Fibre	4g

Preheat the oven to Gas Mark 4/180°C/350°F. Heat the oil in a large frying pan and fry the aubergine (eggplant) slices, in batches if necessary, until well browned on both sides. Arrange half of them in an ovenproof casserole, put the lamb on top and cover with the tomatoes. Sprinkle generously with the marjoram and some salt and pepper, then cover with the remaining aubergine (eggplant). Purée the sunflower and sesame seeds in a food processor with the olive oil, tofu and lemon juice to taste; spoon this mixture over the aubergine (eggplant). Bake for 20–30 minutes or until the top is well browned. Serve at once, garnished with fresh marjoram.

Cassoulet
*gluten and wheat free if breadcrumbs are omitted

DAIRY AND EGG FREE; NO ADDED SUGAR

SERVES FOUR

PREPARATION
AND COOKING
TIME:
3 HOURS +
SOAKING

250g (8 oz/1 cup) dried haricot (great Northern) beans
6 rashers of streaky bacon
2 carrots, sliced
2 onions, stuck with 4 cloves, plus 1 large onion, chopped roughly
2 garlic cloves, peeled and halved
6–8 peppercorns
2 tablespoons olive or vegetable oil
125g (4 oz/1 cup) garlic sausage, diced (*check ingredients for your allergenic food*)
500g (1 lb) shoulder of lamb, cubed
1 tablespoon tomato purée (paste)
600 ml (1 pint/2½ cups) chicken stock (bouillon) (*see page 3*)
125g (4 oz/1 cup) brown breadcrumbs (*optional*)
sea salt

PER PORTION	
Kcal	840
Kjoules	3490
Protein	53g
Tot. fat	51g
Sat. fat	13g
MUFA	17g
PUFA	4g
Carb.	44g
of which tot. sugar	11g
Fibre	17g

Soak the beans in cold water for at least 4 hours, then drain.
Preheat the oven to Gas Mark 3/160°C/325°F. Line a large casserole dish with the bacon. Mix together the beans, carrots, onions stuck with cloves, garlic, peppercorns and a little salt. Spoon this mixture into the casserole, add water to cover, and bake, covered, for 2 hours. Meanwhile, heat the oil in a pan and brown the garlic sausage and the lamb. Stir in the chopped onion, tomato purée (paste) and stock (bouillon). Bring to the boil and simmer

gently for 30 minutes, then add it to the bean pot, stir well to combine and return the dish to the oven for 30 minutes. Taste and adjust the seasoning if necessary.

If you are not using the breadcrumbs, serve the cassoulet straight away. Otherwise, sprinkle the breadcrumbs over the top in a thick layer and return the dish to the oven, uncovered, for 20–25 minutes, until the crumbs are crisp. Serve at once.

Braised Lamb with Vegetables

DAIRY, GLUTEN, WHEAT AND EGG FREE; NO ADDED SUGAR

SERVES FOUR

PREPARATION
AND COOKING
TIME:
1¼ HOURS

750g–1kg (1½–2 lb) joint of lamb, such as
shoulder or half leg
4 garlic cloves, peeled
2 tablespoons olive or vegetable oil
250g (8 oz/2 cups) leeks, sliced
25g (8 oz/1¾ cups) sweet potatoes or ordinary
potatoes, parboiled, then peeled and sliced thickly
2 large or 4 small tomatoes, sliced
175g (6 oz/3 cups) broccoli florets
150 ml (¼ pint/⅔ cup) dry white wine or
vegetable stock (bouillon) (see page 2)
sea salt and freshly ground black pepper

PER PORTION	
Kcal	380
Kjoules	1580
Protein	28g
Tot. fat	20g
Sat. fat	7g
MUFA	10g
PUFA	2g
Carb.	17g
of which tot. sugar	7g
Fibre	4g

Preheat the oven to Gas Mark 4/180°C/350°F.
Cut four deep slits in the lamb and insert the
garlic cloves.

Pour the oil into a fairly deep ovenproof dish
large enough to hold all the vegetables and
the meat. Scatter the leeks over the dish and
cover them with the sliced potatoes, then
season generously with salt and pepper. Lay
the tomatoes on top of the potatoes then put
the joint of lamb on top and arrange the
broccoli florets around it. Season again and
pour the wine or stock (bouillon) over the
top. Cover the dish and bake for 40–55
minutes, depending on whether you like
your lamb pink or well cooked.

Serve straight from the dish.

Pork and Parsnip Bake

SERVES FOUR

PREPARATION AND COOKING TIME: 1¼ HOURS

4 pork chops, trimmed of their fat
2 tablespoons olive or vegetable oil
500g (1 lb/10 cups) parsnips, sliced thinly
250g (8 oz/4 cups) fresh spinach
2 medium cooking apples, peeled, cored and sliced
sea salt and freshly ground black pepper

Preheat the oven to Gas Mark 4/180°C/350°F. Lightly fry the pork chops in the oil until browned and then set them aside.

Brush a little of the oil from the frying pan over the base of an ovenproof casserole. Lay half the parsnips in the bottom, season lightly and lay the pork chops on top.

Mix the spinach and apples together, season lightly and spoon them over the pork. Arrange the remaining parsnips over the top. Cover the dish and bake for 30 minutes, then remove the lid, brush the parsnips with the remaining cooking oil and cook for a further 15 minutes to brown the top slightly.

PER PORTION	
Kcal	345
Kjoules	1450
Protein	25g
Tot. fat	17g
Sat. fat	4g
MUFA	9g
PUFA	3g
Carb.	26g
of which tot. sugar	17g
Fibre	10g

Pineapple Chicken

SERVES FOUR

**PREPARATION
AND COOKING
TIME:
I HOUR**

4 chicken joints
I large onion, sliced thinly in rings
I teaspoon fresh rosemary
I teaspoon sea salt
½ teaspoon ground ginger
a pinch each of black pepper and paprika
400 ml (14 fl oz/1¾ cups) unsweetened pineapple juice

Preheat the oven to Gas Mark 4/180°C/350°F. Place the chicken joints in an ovenproof dish and sprinkle over the onion rings, rosemary, salt, ginger, pepper and paprika. Pour over the pineapple juice and bake, uncovered, for about 45 minutes or until the chicken is cooked through and brown on the top.
Serve with brown rice.

PER PORTION	
Kcal	240
Kjoules	1000
Protein	32g
Tot. fat	7g
Sat. fat	2g
MUFA	3g
PUFA	1g
Carb.	14g
of which tot. sugar	13g
Fibre	1g

Pasta Primavera

*dairy free if cheese is omitted; gluten and egg free, depending on pasta used

WHEAT FREE; NO ADDED SUGAR

SERVES FOUR

PREPARATION
AND COOKING
TIME:
30 MINUTES

3 tablespoons olive or vegetable oil
2 leeks, sliced very thinly
4 celery sticks, chopped very finely
125g (4 oz/1⅓ cups) mushrooms, sliced thinly
200g (7 oz/2 cups) canned artichoke hearts, drained and quartered
50g (2 oz/¼ cup) ham or tongue, chopped
300 ml (½ pint/1⅓ cups) soya cream or silken tofu, puréed
150 ml (¼ pint/⅔ cup) dry white wine or vegetable stock (bouillon) (see page 2)
juice of ½–1 lemon
500g (1 lb/5⅓ cups) noodles, gluten and wheat-free pasta or egg-free rice noodles
a handful of fresh parsley, chopped
sea salt and freshly ground black pepper
flat-leaf parsley, to garnish

PER PORTION	
Kcal	650
Kjoules	2750
Protein	25g
Tot. fat	24g
Sat. fat	5g
MUFA	12g
PUFA	4g
Carb.	83g
of which tot. sugar	4g
Fibre	8g

Heat the oil in a heavy pan and gently cook the leeks and celery until soft; add the mushrooms and continue to cook for a few minutes. Add the artichoke hearts and ham or tongue. Stir in the soya cream or tofu and the wine or stock (bouillon), mix well and simmer for a few minutes.

Add the lemon juice to taste and then season. Cook the noodles in plenty of fast-boiling water until just tender, then drain quickly and transfer to a dish. Stir the parsley into the sauce, spoon it over the noodles and serve immediately, garnished with flat-leaf parsley.

Stir-Fries

SERVES FOUR

PREPARATION
AND COOKING
TIME:
30 MINUTES

1 kg (2 lb/8 cups) mixed vegetables – ready-mixed packs of vegetables for stir-frying are now available; juicy vegetables such as cucumber and beansprouts are particularly good
2 tablespoons oil, such as rapeseed or groundnut
1 teaspoon finely chopped garlic
1 teaspoon finely chopped fresh ginger root or fresh turmeric root
250g (8 oz/1 cup) protein-rich food – cooked ham, chicken, smoked mackerel, prawns (shrimp), etc., or, for a vegetarian stir-fry, nuts (cashews, peanuts, flaked almonds) or seeds (sunflower, pumpkin or sesame)
gluten and wheat-free soy sauce (*check the label for sugar*)
sea salt and freshly ground black pepper

Cut the vegetables into thin slices or matchsticks, leaving beansprouts whole. Root vegetables must be sliced very thinly.
Heat the oil in a wok or a large frying pan until nearly smoking. Add the garlic and the ginger or turmeric and cook for a few minutes, stirring constantly. Add any harder vegetables, such as carrots and other root vegetables, turn the heat down slightly and cook for 5 minutes or until the vegetables are just beginning to soften.
Add softer vegetables, such as peppers, mush-rooms and broccoli, turn the heat up again

and cook briskly for 2 minutes, stirring constantly.

Add the protein food of your choice (you can brown nuts first in the oven or on a dry frying pan for extra flavour), then season with soy sauce and salt and pepper to taste.

Serve at once.

Barbecues
*dairy free if dairy yoghurt is omitted from marinade

SERVES FOUR

PREPARATION
AND COOKING
TIME:
45 MINUTES

Allow 250g (8 oz/1 cup) per person of any of the following:

meat, such as pork, beef, lamb or poultry, cut into fairly large cubes

fish, preferably solid fish such as tuna, mackerel, shark or shellfish (soft, white fish disintegrates), in steaks or cut into large cubes

vegetables, a selection of juicy vegetables, such as celery, peppers, tomatoes, mushrooms and courgettes (zucchini), or root vegetables

fruit, firm fresh fruit, such as banana and pineapple, and plump dried fruit

plus: 1 baking potato per person

For the Marinade:
4 tablespoons olive, sunflower, rapeseed or soya (canola) oil
2 tablespoons lemon juice or vinegar
2 tablespoons dairy or soya yoghurt (*optional*)
sea salt and freshly ground black pepper
plus any of the following flavouring ingredients, to taste:
crushed garlic, tomato purée (paste), chopped fresh ginger root, dried herbs and spices, wine

Mix together all the ingredients for the marinade.
Thread cubes of meat or fish on to skewers and marinate for about 2 hours to tenderise them and keep them moist.

Vegetables and fruit can be left whole or cut into chunks and threaded on kebab skewers. Root vegetables should be parboiled before barbecuing, while juicy vegetables can be placed straight on the barbecue. Brush vegetables with a little oil or marinade both before and during cooking.

If you like your meat well done, cook it first, then add any fish, vegetables and fruit; if rare, cook them all together. Turn often to prevent burning and baste continually with the marinade or oil.

Microwave the baking potatoes for a few minutes and then finish them on the barbecue.

Penne Paesana

*dairy free if cheese is omitted; gluten and egg free, depending on pasta used

SERVES FOUR

PREPARATION
AND COOKING
TIME:
30 MINUTES

about 2 tablespoons olive or sunflower oil
1 large onion, chopped finely
250g (8 oz/2 cups) small courgettes (zucchini), sliced
175g (6 oz/1½ cups) aubergine (eggplant), diced finely
250g (8 oz/2 cups) tomatoes, chopped
50g (2 oz/¼ cup) ham, chopped
125 ml (4 fl oz/½ cup) dry white wine or vegetable stock (bouillon) (see page 2)
1 tablespoon fresh basil or 1 teaspoon dried
500g (1 lb/5⅓ cups) fresh penne, gluten and wheat-free pasta or egg-free rice noodles
sea salt and freshly ground black pepper
shavings of Parmesan cheese, to serve (optional)

PER PORTION	
Kcal	620
Kjoules	2620
Protein	17g
Tot. fat	16g
Sat. fat	2g
MUFA	8g
PUFA	5g
Carb.	103g
of which tot. sugar	10g
Fibre	9g

Heat the oil in a pan and gently fry the onion until it is just beginning to soften.

Add the courgettes (zucchini) and aubergine (eggplant) and cook for a few minutes.

Next add the tomatoes, ham and wine or stock (bouillon) and stir well. Cover and simmer for about 10 minutes or until the vegetables are just tender. Season to taste and add the basil if you are using dried basil.

Cook the pasta in plenty of fast-boiling water until it is just tender. Drain thoroughly, stir in a little extra oil and serve topped with the sauce and sprinkled with the fresh basil and Parmesan cheese, if used.

Vegetarian Dishes

Many of these dishes are in fact vegan – a boon to food intolerants, since they contain no animal or dairy products and no eggs. Even for coeliacs, vegetarian dishes, with their liberal use of gluten-free pulses (legumes), rice and grains such as quinoa, offer some interesting possibilities.

Cracked Wheat with Spinach and Pine (Pignolia) Kernels

SERVES FOUR

PREPARATION AND COOKING TIME: 30 MINUTES

4 tablespoons olive or sunflower oil
75g (3 oz/1 cup) okra, chopped finely
½ heaped teaspoon ground cumin
125g (4 oz/1 cup) mushrooms, sliced
75g (3 oz/1½ cups) fresh spinach, chopped
6 heaped tablespoons cracked wheat
225 ml (7½ fl oz/1 cup) boiling water
125 ml (4 fl oz/½ cup) dry white wine
40g (1½ oz/⅓ cup) raisins
75g (3 oz/¾ cup) mangetout (snowpeas), chopped quite finely
25g (1 oz/⅕ cup) pine (pignolia) kernels
juice of ½ lemon
sea salt and freshly ground black pepper

PER PORTION	
Kcal	400
Kjoules	1670
Protein	8g
Tot. fat	21g
Sat. fat	3g
MUFA	12g
PUFA	5g
Carb.	43g
of which tot. sugar	9g
Fibre	4g

Heat the oil in a large pan and gently cook the okra and cumin for 2 minutes.
Add the mushrooms and spinach and cook for a few minutes until both are wilted.
Meanwhile, put the cracked wheat in a bowl, pour over the boiling water and leave for about 5 minutes, until swollen. If the wheat is not soft enough, add a little more water and leave a few minutes longer.
Add the cracked wheat, wine, and raisins to the mushrooms and spinach and cook for a few minutes longer. If the mixture is dry, stir in a little more wine or water. Finally add the mangetout (snowpeas), pine (pignolia) kernels and lemon juice and season to taste. Serve at once, accompanied by a green salad.

Autumn Bean Stew

DAIRY, GLUTEN, WHEAT AND EGG FREE; NO ADDED SUGAR

SERVES FOUR

PREPARATION AND COOKING TIME: 45 MINUTES

2 tablespoons vegetable oil
1 garlic clove, crushed
125g (4 oz/1 cup) onions, chopped finely
125g (4 oz/1 cup) mushrooms, chopped roughly
50g (2 oz/½ cup) celery, chopped roughly
40g (1½ oz/¼ cup) tomato purée (paste)
175g (6 oz/¾ cup) canned tomatoes
a pinch each of dried thyme, parsley and sage
175g (6 oz/1 cup) canned red kidney beans
(*check the label for sugar*)
175g (6 oz/1 cup) canned butter (lima) beans
(*check the label for sugar*)
175g (6 oz/1 cup) canned chickpeas (garbanzo beans) (*check the label for sugar*)
250 ml (8 fl oz/1 cup) vegetable stock (bouillon) (see page 2)
125g (4 oz/2 cups) savoy cabbage, sliced thinly
275g (9 oz/2¼ cups) smoked tofu, cubed
sea salt and freshly ground black pepper

PER PORTION	
Kcal	270
Kjoules	1150
Protein	17g
Tot. fat	11g
Sat. fat	1g
MUFA	3g
PUFA	5g
Carb.	28g
of which tot. sugar	8g
Fibre	7g

Heat the oil in a deep, heavy pan and add the garlic, onions, mushrooms and celery. Cook gently for 5-10 minutes, until starting to soften. Add the tomato purée (paste), canned tomatoes, herbs, beans, chickpeas (garbanzo beans) and vegetable stock (bouillon). Bring to the boil, then reduce the heat and simmer gently for 10 minutes. Add the cabbage and tofu and simmer for another 10 minutes or until the cabbage is cooked but still slightly crunchy. Season to taste and then serve.

Potato and Polenta Bake with Apple Sauce

GLUTEN, WHEAT AND EGG FREE

SERVES FOUR

**PREPARATION
AND COOKING
TIME:
1¼ HOURS**

For the Bake:

750g (1½ lb/5 cups) floury old potatoes, diced (*do not peel*)
250g (8 oz/1¼ cups) quick-cooking coarse polenta
450 ml (¾ pint/2 cups) milk
300 ml (½ pint/1⅓ cups) water
250g (8 oz/2 cups) Gorgonzola or dolcelatte cheese, grated or diced very finely
1 teaspoon dried mixed herbs
25g (1 oz/⅛ cup) butter or 2 tablespoons olive oil
sea salt and freshly ground black pepper

For the Sauce:

750g (1½ lb/6 cups) cooking apples, peeled, cored and chopped
5 cloves
1 teaspoon cinnamon
50g (2 oz/¼ cup) granulated sugar
125 ml (4 fl oz/½ cup) water

PER PORTION	
Kcal	880
Kjoules	3690
Protein	24g
Tot. fat	38g
Sat. fat	20g
MUFA	14g
PUFA	13g
Carb.	113g
of which tot. sugar	36g
Fibre	10g

Preheat the oven to Gas Mark 4/180°C/350°F. Boil the potatoes until they are almost mushy, then drain and set aside.

Put the polenta, milk and water in a pan and cook gently for 15–20 minutes, stirring constantly, until most of the liquid has been absorbed. Season generously and then mix in the cheese and herbs.

Mix the polenta with the potatoes, mashing the potatoes first if you prefer a smoother texture, and pile the mixture into an ovenproof dish. Dot the top with the butter or drizzle over the oil and bake for 30 minutes. Meanwhile, put the apples in a pan with the cloves, cinnamon, sugar and water and cook gently until tender. Remove the cloves and purée or sieve the apples, then reheat gently. Serve the bake accompanied by the apple sauce.

Red Cabbage and Apple Casserole

SERVES FOUR

PREPARATION AND COOKING TIME: I HOUR

I large onion, chopped roughly
I bulb of fennel, chopped roughly
375g (12 oz/6 cups) red cabbage, sliced thinly
I cooking apple, peeled, cored and chopped
I heaped teaspoon caraway seeds
2 teaspoons creamed horseradish (*check the label for gluten and sugar*)
250 ml (8 fl oz/I cup) yoghurt
sea salt and freshly ground black pepper

Preheat the oven to Gas Mark 3/160°C/325°F.
Mix together the onion, fennel, cabbage, apple and caraway seeds in a bowl.
Mix the horseradish with the yoghurt, season lightly with salt and pepper and stir it into the vegetables. Transfer the mixture to an ovenproof casserole and bake for 45–50 minutes, stir once or twice during cooking. The cabbage should still be slightly crisp at the end of cooking.
Serve hot with rye bread, if you can eat it, or boiled potatoes.

PER PORTION	
Kcal	100
Kjoules	435
Protein	8g
Tot. fat	2g
Sat. fat	Ig
MUFA	Ig
PUFA	neg
Carb.	15g
of which tot. sugar	13g
Fibre	4g

Mushroom and Nut Risotto

SERVES FOUR

PREPARATION AND COOKING TIME: 45 MINUTES

2 tablespoons olive, nut or vegetable oil
1 small onion, chopped finely
1 celery stick, chopped finely
1 head of chicory, chopped finely
250g (8 oz/2 cups) large flat mushrooms, chopped finely
175g (6 oz/¾ cup) brown rice
150 ml (¼ pint/⅔ cup) dry white wine
150 ml (¼ pint/⅔ cup) water
juice of ½–1 lemon
50g (2 oz/⅓ cup) walnuts or cashew nuts, chopped
sea salt and freshly ground black pepper

PER PORTION	
Kcal	350
Kjoules	1470
Protein	6g
Tot. fat	18g
Sat. fat	2g
MUFA	7g
PUFA	7g
Carb.	39g
of which tot. sugar	3g
Fibre	4g

Heat the oil in a wide pan and gently fry the onion, celery and chicory until they are beginning to brown. Raise the heat, add the mushrooms and cook for several minutes.
Add the rice, cook for 1–2 minutes, then stir in the wine and water. Reduce the heat, cover and simmer for about 20 minutes or until the liquid has been absorbed and the rice is cooked. Add extra water if the liquid is absorbed too quickly.
Add lemon juice to taste and season with salt and pepper. Just before serving, stir in the nuts.

Bean Bourguignon

DAIRY, GLUTEN, WHEAT AND EGG FREE; NO ADDED SUGAR

SERVES SIX

PREPARATION
AND COOKING
TIME:
1 HOUR

2 tablespoons vegetable oil
2 garlic cloves, crushed
175g (6 oz/1½ cups) button onions, peeled
75g (3 oz/¾ cup) celery, diced
75g (3 oz/¾ cup) red pepper, sliced thinly
175g (6 oz/¾ cup) small button mushrooms
1 teaspoon dried thyme
1 teaspoon dried parsley
2 bay leaves
¼ teaspoon black peppercorns
25g (1 oz/⅕ cup) cornflour (cornstarch)
250 ml (8 fl oz/1 cup) red wine
250 ml (8 fl oz/1 cup) vegetable stock (bouillon)
(see page 2)
439g (14 oz/2 cups) can of butter (lima) beans
(check the label for sugar)
175g (6 oz/⅔ cup) canned flageolet beans (check
the label for sugar)
125g (4 oz/½ cup) canned cannellini beans (check
the label for sugar)
sea salt

PER PORTION	
Kcal	310
Kjoules	1320
Protein	13g
Tot. fat	9g
Sat. fat	1g
MUFA	3g
PUFA	4g
Carb.	37g
of which tot. sugar	6g
Fibre	5g

Heat the oil in a heavy-based pan and gently
cook the garlic, onions, celery and red pepper
until softened but not brown.

Add the mushrooms, herbs and peppercorns,
cook for a few more minutes, then stir in the
cornflour (cornstarch). Add the red wine and
stock (bouillon) and season lightly. Bring back
to the boil and simmer gently for 30 minutes.

Add the beans and gradually bring back to the
boil again; adjust the seasoning to taste and
then serve.

Baked Fennel with Spinach and Root Vegetables *dairy free if yoghurt omitted

GLUTEN, WHEAT AND EGG FREE; NO ADDED SUGAR

SERVES FOUR

PREPARATION AND COOKING TIME: 1½ HOURS

1kg (2 lb/6½ cups) parsnips, celeriac, sweet potatoes, or any combination of these vegetables, chopped
250g (8 oz/⅔ cup) potatoes, chopped
a little olive oil
1 large banana
50g (2 oz/½ cup) pumpkin seeds
500g (1 lb/8 cups) cooked fresh or frozen leaf spinach
2 large bulbs of fennel, cut in half lengthways
juice of 1 lemon
½ teaspoon gluten and wheat-free soy sauce (*check the label for sugar*)
½ teaspoon turmeric
150 ml (¼ pint/⅔ cup) live yoghurt or silken tofu
1 tablespoon sesame seeds
sea salt and freshly ground black pepper

PER PORTION	
Kcal	430
Kjoules	1820
Protein	14g
Tot. fat	14g
Sat. fat	2g
MUFA	5g
PUFA	6g
Carb.	67g
of which tot. sugar	25g
Fibre	14g

Preheat the oven to Gas Mark 4/180°C/350°F. Steam the parsnips, celeriac, sweet potatoes and potatoes until soft, then mash them with a little olive oil and some seasoning to taste. Put them in an ovenproof casserole dish and slice the banana over them.

Mix the pumpkin seeds with the cooked spinach, season to taste and spread this mixture over the banana.

Steam the fennel until soft but still holding its shape. Place the fennel halves, cut-side down, on top of the spinach.

Mix the lemon juice, soy sauce and turmeric together and add to the yoghurt or silken tofu. Season to taste and pour it over the fennel. Sprinkle over the sesame seeds and bake, covered, for 35 minutes, or microwave in a 650/750-watt oven on full power for 4 minutes.

Root Vegetable Casserole

DAIRY, GLUTEN, WHEAT AND EGG FREE; NO ADDED SUGAR

SERVES FOUR

PREPARATION AND COOKING TIME: 45 MINUTES

1kg (2 lb/8 cups) mixed root vegetables, such as parsnip, carrot, swede or turnip, chopped
397g (14 oz/2 cups) can of tomatoes
2 teaspoons dried mixed herbs
sea salt and freshly ground black pepper

Put all the ingredients in a pan. Cover, bring to the boil, then reduce the heat and simmer gently for 30 minutes or until the vegetables are cooked.

Adjust the seasoning to taste before serving.

PER PORTION	
Kcal	110
Kjoules	470
Protein	4g
Tot. fat	1g
Sat. fat	neg
MUFA	neg
PUFA	neg
Carb.	22g
of which tot. sugar	17g
Fibre	8g

Potato, Leek and Apple Pie

DAIRY, GLUTEN, WHEAT AND EGG FREE; NO ADDED SUGAR

SERVES FOUR

PREPARATION
AND COOKING
TIME:
I HOUR

2 tablespoons olive oil
1kg (2 lb/6½ cups) potatoes, sliced thickly
2 leeks, sliced thickly
375g (12 oz/6 cups) white cabbage, sliced finely
1 large cooking apple, peeled, cored and sliced
3 tablespoons sesame seeds (*optional*)
sea salt and freshly ground black pepper

Preheat the oven to Gas Mark 4/180°C/350°F.
Steam the potato slices until half cooked.
Pour the oil into a large ovenproof dish and
arrange half the potatoes in the bottom.
Mix together the sliced leeks, cabbage and
apples, season lightly with salt and pepper and
arrange over the potatoes. Cover with the
remaining potatoes and add water to the dish
to a depth of about 1 cm (½ inch). Sprinkle
the sesame seeds over the potatoes, if used,
and bake for 30–40 minutes or until the
potatoes are cooked and the seeds are nicely
browned.

PER PORTION	
Kcal	370
Kjoules	1540
Protein	9g
Tot. fat	15g
Sat. fat	2g
MUFA	8g
PUFA	4g
Carb.	52g
of which tot. sugar	10g
Fibre	8g

Mushroom and Sunflower Seed Flan
* gluten and wheat free if gluten-free pastry is used

DAIRY AND EGG FREE; NO ADDED SUGAR

SERVES FOUR

PREPARATION
AND COOKING
TIME:
45 MINUTES

For the Pastry:
75g (3 oz/⅓ cup) dairy-free margarine
175g (6 oz/1⅓ cups) wholemeal flour
or use gluten-free pastry (see *page 108*)

For the Filling:
3 tablespoons olive oil
175g (6 oz/¾ cup) baby sweetcorn (corn), each
cut in half lengthways
2 heaped tablespoons sunflower seeds
250g (8 oz/2 cups) mushrooms, whole, halved or
quartered
75g (3 oz/1½ cups) fresh spinach, chopped quite
finely
sea salt and freshly ground black pepper

PER PORTION	
Kcal	440
Kjoules	1840
Protein	10g
Tot. fat	32g
Sat. fat	7g
MUFA	15g
PUFA	8g
Carb.	31g
of which tot. sugar	2g
Fibre	6g

Preheat the oven to Gas Mark 4/180°C/350°F.
If you are making the pastry, rub the margarine
into the flour then add enough water to make
a firm dough. Roll out this dough or the
gluten-free pastry and use it to line a 20 cm
(8-inch) flan dish. Prick the bottom, line it
with foil or greaseproof paper, weight it with
beans or rice and bake blind (empty) for about
15 minutes. Remove the foil and beans or rice,
then bake for a further 10 minutes, until crisp.
Meanwhile, heat the oil in a heavy pan and
add the sweetcorn (corn) and sunflower seeds.
Fry briskly until lightly browned, then add the
mushrooms, reduce the heat slightly and cook
for 2 minutes.

Stir in the chopped spinach, cover the pan and cook for 2 more minutes.
Season well and spoon the filling into the flan case. Serve hot, warm or cold.

Beetroot (Beet), Artichoke and Ginger Stir-Fry

DAIRY, GLUTEN, WHEAT AND EGG FREE; NO ADDED SUGAR

SERVES FOUR

PREPARATION AND COOKING TIME: 30 MINUTES

375g (12 oz/2 cups) raw beetroot (beet), cut into matchsticks
375g (12 oz/2 cups) Jerusalem artichokes, cut into matchsticks
3 tablespoons sunflower oil
2 large garlic cloves, crushed
25g (1 oz/¼ cup) fresh ginger root, peeled and shredded
50g (2 oz/½ cup) sunflower seeds
a handful of fresh parsley, chopped
gluten and wheat-free soy sauce, to taste (*check the label for sugar*)

PER PORTION	
Kcal	250
Kjoules	1080
Protein	6g
Tot. fat	18g
Sat. fat	2g
MUFA	4g
PUFA	11g
Carb.	20g
of which tot. sugar	9g
Fibre	3g

Put the beetroot (beet) in a steamer and cook for 5 minutes, then add the Jerusalem artichokes and steam for a further 5–10 minutes or until the vegetables are just cooked but still slightly crisp. (If you do not have a steamer you can cook them in a metal colander over a pan of boiling water, or in a microwave.)

Heat the oil in a frying pan and gently cook the garlic and ginger until soft but not browned. Turn up the heat a little and add the sunflower seeds and steamed vegetables. Cook briskly for 2 minutes, stirring constantly, until the vegetables are heated through. Stir in the parsley, add soy sauce to taste and serve at once.

Rice, Chilli and Bamboo Shoot Casserole

GLUTEN, WHEAT AND EGG FREE; NO ADDED SUGAR

SERVES FOUR

PREPARATION
AND COOKING
TIME:
1¼ HOURS

2 tablespoons olive or sunflower oil
6 large spring onions (scallions), chopped
25g (1 oz/¼ cup) fresh green chillies, de-seeded
and finely sliced
250g (8 oz/1¼ cups) brown rice
600 ml (1 pint/2½ cups) vegetable stock (bouillon)
(see page 2), or a mixture of white wine and
water
375g (12 oz/2 cups) canned bamboo shoots,
drained
200 ml (7 fl oz/¾ cup) low-fat yoghurt
150g (5 oz/1¼ cups) well-flavoured cheese, grated
sea salt and freshly ground black pepper

PER PORTION	
Kcal	540
Kjoules	2250
Protein	18g
Tot. fat	23g
Sat. fat	10g
MUFA	9g
PUFA	2g
Carb.	56g
of which tot. sugar	6g
Fibre	3g

Preheat the oven to Gas Mark 4/180°C/350°F.
Heat the oil in a pan and gently fry the spring
onions (scallions) and chillies until soft. Stir
in the rice, cook for 2 minutes, then add the
liquid. Bring to the boil and simmer for about
20 minutes or until the rice is cooked and
most of the liquid has been absorbed.
Add the bamboo shoots and yoghurt and
season to taste.
Spoon half the mixture into a casserole dish,
sprinkle over half the cheese then cover with
the remaining mixture. Sprinkle over the
remaining cheese and bake for 25 minutes,
until the cheese is melted and lightly browned,
or microwave the casserole in a 650/750 watt
oven on full power for 6 minutes, then brown
the top under the grill (broiler).

Chickpeas (garbanzo beans) with Chillies and Peppers

DAIRY, GLUTEN, WHEAT AND EGG FREE; NO ADDED SUGAR

SERVES FOUR

PREPARATION
AND COOKING
TIME:
30 MINUTES

4 tablespoons olive or vegetable oil
2 onions, chopped roughly
2 garlic cloves, crushed
2 fresh green chillies, chopped
1 red and 2 green peppers, chopped roughly
500g (1 lb/2½ cups) canned chickpeas (garbanzo beans) (*check the label for sugar*)
2 large tomatoes, skinned and chopped
150 ml (¼ pint/⅔ cup) vegetable stock (bouillon) (*see page 2*)
juice of 1 large lemon
sea salt and freshly ground black pepper

Heat the oil in a heavy-based pan and add the onions, garlic, chillies and peppers. Fry them gently for 5 minutes, until softened but not browned then stir in the drained chickpeas (garbanzo beans), plus the tomatoes, stock (bouillon), lemon juice and seasoning to taste. Cover and simmer for 20 minutes, or until the peppers are tender.
Adjust the seasoning to taste and serve either hot or cold.

PER PORTION	
Kcal	310
Kjoules	1300
Protein	10g
Tot. fat	19g
Sat. fat	3g
MUFA	11g
PUFA	4g
Carb.	26g
of which tot. sugar	5g
Fibre	3g

Pepper, Nut and Tofu Stir-Fry

DAIRY, GLUTEN, WHEAT AND EGG FREE; NO ADDED SUGAR

SERVES FOUR

PREPARATION
AND COOKING
TIME:
15 MINUTES

4 tablespoons olive oil
3 large green peppers, sliced
125g (4 oz/¾ cup) nuts, such as cashews, hazelnuts
or peanuts, whole or broken
1 heaped teaspoon coriander seeds
250g (8 oz/2 cups) smoked tofu, diced
gluten and wheat-free soy sauce, to taste (*check
the label for sugar*)

Heat the oil in a pan and gently cook the
green peppers until slightly softened.
Add the nuts and coriander seeds and cook for
5 minutes, until the nuts are lightly browned.
Add the tofu and cook for 2 minutes or until
it is heated through and slightly browned.
Season with soy sauce and serve at once.

PER PORTION	
Kcal	300
Kjoules	1230
Protein	9g
Tot. fat	27g
Sat. fat	4g
MUFA	15g
PUFA	5g
Carb.	7g
of which tot. sugar	1g
Fibre	1g

Spinach Soufflé

SERVES FOUR

**PREPARATION
AND COOKING
TIME:
45 MINUTES**

4 tablespoons olive oil
2 leeks, sliced very finely
125g (4 oz/1 cup) mushrooms, sliced finely
500g (1 lb/8 cups) young spinach leaves, chopped finely
200g (7 oz/2 cups) silken tofu, puréed
5 large egg yolks
6 large egg whites
1 tablespoon sesame seeds
sea salt and freshly ground black pepper

Preheat the oven to Gas Mark 4/180°C/350°F.
Heat the oil in a heavy pan and gently cook the leeks and mushrooms until tender.
Add the spinach, cover and cook until the spinach is reduced almost to a purée. Stir in the silken tofu and season well, then remove from the heat and stir in the egg yolks.
Whisk the egg whites until they just hold their shape in soft peaks. Stir a third of the whites into the spinach mixture and then gently fold in the rest. Pour the mixture into a 1.2-litre (2-pint) soufflé dish, sprinkle over the sesame seeds and bake for 20–25 minutes or until the soufflé is risen and golden. Serve at once.

PER PORTION	
Kcal	360
Kjoules	1500
Protein	19g
Tot. fat	30g
Sat. fat	6g
MUFA	16g
PUFA	6g
Carb.	4g
of which tot. sugar	3g
Fibre	7g

Carrot and Cashew Pilaff

DAIRY, GLUTEN, WHEAT AND EGG FREE; NO ADDED SUGAR

SERVES FOUR

PREPARATION
AND COOKING
TIME:
45 MINUTES

250g (8 oz/⅔ cup) carrots, sliced finely
2 tablespoons olive oil
125g (4 oz/1 cup) onions, chopped very finely
150g (5 oz/⅔ cup) mushrooms, chopped very finely
300g (10 oz/1½ cups) brown basmati rice
900 ml (1½ pints/3¾ cups) vegetable stock (bouillon) (see page 2)
125g (4 oz/¾ cup) broken cashew nuts
gluten and wheat-free soy sauce, to taste (check label for sugar)

Boil or steam the carrots until they are just cooked but still firm. Drain and set aside.
Heat the oil in a pan and gently fry the onions and mushrooms for 5 minutes or until they are starting to soften and brown.
Add the rice, stir for a few minutes, then add the stock (bouillon). Bring to the boil and simmer for 15–20 minutes or until the rice is just cooked and the liquid has been absorbed.
Stir in the cooked carrots and the cashew nuts and season to taste with soy sauce.
Serve at room temperature.

PER PORTION	
Kcal	550
Kjoules	2290
Protein	12g
Tot. fat	24g
Sat. fat	4g
MUFA	13g
PUFA	6g
Carb.	76g
of which tot. sugar	7g
Fibre	6g

Okra and Potato Stew

DAIRY, GLUTEN, WHEAT AND EGG FREE; NO ADDED SUGAR

SERVES FOUR

PREPARATION
AND COOKING
TIME:
45 MINUTES

625g (1¼ lb/4 cups) waxy potatoes, diced quite finely
1 tablespoon vegetable oil
50g (2 oz/½ cup) onion, chopped
200g (7 oz/2 cups) okra, sliced
100g (3½ oz/2⅓ cups) canned tomatoes
Tabasco sauce, to taste
15g (½ oz/⅒ cup) cornflour (cornstarch)
150 ml (¼ pint/⅔ cup) vegetable stock (bouillon) (see page 2)
sea salt and freshly ground black pepper

Boil or steam the potatoes until they are just cooked, then drain and set aside.

Heat the oil in a pan and fry the onion and okra for a few minutes until they start to soften. Add the tomatoes and a good shake of Tabasco sauce and continue to cook for 5 minutes.

Mix the cornflour (cornstarch) with a little of the vegetable stock (bouillon) to make a smooth paste, then add it to the pan with the rest of the stock (bouillon) and the potatoes. Bring back to the boil and simmer gently for 10 minutes. Season to taste.

PER PORTION	
Kcal	190
Kjoules	800
Protein	5g
Tot. fat	5g
Sat. fat	1g
MUFA	1g
PUFA	2g
Carb.	34g
of which tot. sugar	4g
Fibre	5g

Mixed Vegetables with Carrot and Onion Purée *dairy free if cheese is omitted

GLUTEN, WHEAT AND EGG FREE; NO ADDED SUGAR

SERVES FOUR

PREPARATION
AND COOKING
TIME:
45 MINUTES

400 ml (14 fl oz/1¾ cups) vegetable stock (bouillon) (see page 2)
175g (6 oz/1½ cups) carrots, chopped roughly
175g (6 oz/1½ cups) onions, chopped roughly
250g (8 oz/2 cups) parsnips, sliced thickly
250g (8 oz/2 cups) waxy potatoes, sliced thickly
125g (4 oz/1 cup) leeks, sliced thickly
125g (4 oz/1 cup) courgettes (zucchini), sliced
125g (4 oz/1 cup) fresh or frozen French beans, sliced
75g (3 oz/¾ cup) sweetcorn (corn)
50g (2 oz/1 cup) Parmesan cheese, grated, or sesame seeds
sea salt and freshly ground black pepper

PER PORTION	
Kcal	210
Kjoules	900
Protein	10g
Tot. fat	6g
Sat. fat	3g
MUFA	2g
PUFA	1g
Carb.	31g
of which tot. sugar	12g
Fibre	8g

Put the vegetable stock (bouillon) into a saucepan, add the carrots and onions and bring to the boil. Simmer for 25 minutes or until tender, then purée in a liquidiser or food processor.

Meanwhile, steam the parsnips, potatoes and leeks together for about 15 minutes or until they are almost tender, then add the courgettes (zucchini) and French beans and continue to steam until all the vegetables are cooked. Stir the sweetcorn (corn) into the onion and carrot purée and season to taste. Put the steamed vegetables into a serving dish and pour over the vegetable purée. Top with the grated Parmesan or sesame seeds and serve at once.

Indian Lentils with Sunflower Seeds

SERVES FOUR

PREPARATION AND COOKING TIME:

45 MINUTES

2 tablespoons vegetable oil

125g (4 oz/1 cup) onions, chopped finely

125g (4 oz/1 cup) carrots, diced finely

1 garlic clove, crushed

125g (4 oz/1 cup) mushrooms, chopped finely

½ teaspoon dried parsley

½ teaspoon cumin seeds

½ teaspoon garam masala

150g (5 oz/¾ cup) green lentils

150g (5 oz/¾ cup) red lentils

500 ml (18 fl oz/2⅓ cup) vegetable stock (bouillon) (see page 2)

125g (4 oz/1 cup) sunflower seeds

125g (4 oz/¾ cup) frozen peas

sea salt and freshly ground black pepper

PER PORTION	
Kcal	530
Kjoules	2220
Protein	27g
Tot. fat	24g
Sat. fat	2g
MUFA	6g
PUFA	14g
Carb.	53g
of which tot. sugar	7g
Fibre	8g

Heat the oil in a pan and gently cook the onions, carrots, garlic and mushrooms for 5 minutes.

Add the parsley, cumin seeds and garam masala and continue to cook for 2 minutes. Add the green and red lentils and the vegetable stock (bouillon), bring to the boil and simmer for about 30 minutes or until the lentils are cooked and the liquid has been absorbed. Add a little more stock (bouillon) if necessary.

Stir in the sunflower seeds and peas. Cook for a few minutes until the peas are tender and then season to taste.

Spiced Rice with Green Peas and Pumpkin Seeds

SERVES FOUR

**PREPARATION
AND COOKING
TIME:
30 MINUTES**

1 tablespoon olive or vegetable oil
1 dried chilli, chopped finely
a pinch of cumin seeds
250g (8 oz/1 cup) long-grain white rice
900 ml (1½ pints/3¾ cups) vegetable stock
(bouillon) (see page 2)
250 ml (8 fl oz/1 cup) yoghurt
250g (8 oz/1 cup) cottage cheese
1 tablespoon pumpkin seeds
50g (2 oz/⅔ cup) French beans, chopped
125g (4 oz/¾ cup) frozen peas
sea salt

PER PORTION	
Kcal	420
Kjoules	1760
Protein	20g
Tot. fat	11g
Sat. fat	3g
MUFA	4g
PUFA	2g
Carb.	64g
of which tot. sugar	7g
Fibre	4g

Heat the oil in a frying pan and add the chilli, cumin seeds and rice. Cook gently for 2 minutes, then add half the stock (bouillon). Simmer, uncovered, for 10 minutes then gradually add more stock (bouillon) and continue to cook until the rice is just tender and the liquid has been absorbed.

Stir in the yoghurt, cottage cheese, pumpkin seeds, French beans and peas and continue to cook until everything is heated through.

Add salt to taste and serve warm or at room temperature.

Rice with Apricots

SERVES FOUR

**PREPARATION
AND COOKING
TIME:
40 MINUTES**

1 tablespoon vegetable oil
75g (3 oz/¾ cup) onion, chopped very finely
2 celery sticks, chopped very finely
250g (8 oz/1 cup) brown rice
900 ml (1½ pints/3¾ cups) water
50g (2 oz/¼ cup) dried apricots, chopped
juice of 1 large orange
4 sprigs of fresh parsley, chopped
sea salt and freshly ground black pepper

Heat the oil in a large pan and gently cook
the onion and celery until softened.
Add the rice and stir for 2 minutes, then add
the water. Bring to the boil and cook for about
20 minutes or until the rice is tender and the
water has been absorbed; if necessary add a
little more water during the cooking.
Stir in the apricots (if they are rather dry, add
them half way through the cooking process
to soften them), orange juice, parsley and
seasoning to taste. Serve at once.

PER PORTION	
Kcal	300
Kjoules	1270
Protein	5g
Tot. fat	6g
Sat. fat	1g
MUFA	2g
PUFA	2g
Carb.	60g
of which tot. sugar	10g
Fibre	6g

Salads and Side Dishes

A salad is all too often the only choice available if you have to shun pastry, avoid cream sauces and stay clear of eggs. However, with a little imagination a salad can be not only safe and nutritious but unusual and exciting as well.

Cabbage Braised with Plums
*no added sugar if honey is omitted

DAIRY, GLUTEN, WHEAT AND EGG FREE

SERVES FOUR

PREPARATION
AND COOKING
TIME:
30 MINUTES

2 tablespoons olive or vegetable oil
2 onions, chopped roughly
1 carrot, diced
1 turnip or parsnip, diced
1 cooking apple, peeled and diced
175g (6 oz/1 cup) plums, stoned (pitted) and sliced
1 tablespoon honey (*optional*)
a handful of fresh mixed herbs, chopped, or
1 tablespoon dried herbs
50g (2 oz/1 cup) white cabbage, sliced finely
75g (3 oz/¾ cup) courgette (zucchini), sliced
sea salt and freshly ground black pepper

Heat the oil in a large pan and then add the onions, carrot, turnip or parsnip, apple, plums and honey, if used. Sauté lightly for 2 minutes, then cover and cook gently until the vegetables are beginning to soften, adding a little water if the mixture seems dry. Add the herbs, cabbage and courgette (zucchini) and continue to cook for 10 minutes. Season to taste, then transfer the mixture to a dish and serve hot or cold.

PER PORTION	
Kcal	130
Kjoules	520
Protein	2g
Tot. fat	8g
Sat. fat	1g
MUFA	5g
PUFA	1g
Carb.	13g
of which tot. sugar	11g
Fibre	3g

Stuffed Courgettes (Zucchini)

SERVES FOUR

PREPARATION
AND COOKING
TIME:
30 MINUTES
+ MARINATING

4 courgettes (zucchini)
1 onion, chopped very finely
1 garlic clove, crushed
4 tablespoons French dressing (see page 10)
½ green pepper, chopped finely
2 tomatoes, skinned, de-seeded and chopped finely
½ tablespoon capers
1 teaspoon chopped fresh parsley
1 teaspoon chopped fresh basil
sea salt and freshly ground black pepper

Trim the courgettes (zucchini) and simmer them in boiling salted water until they are half cooked – 2 minutes should be enough. Cut them in half lengthways, scoop out the flesh and chop it.

Sprinkle half the onion, the garlic and some of the dressing over the courgette (zucchini) shells and leave to marinate for about 2 hours. Mix the remaining onion with the green pepper, tomatoes, capers, parsley and basil and stir in the chopped courgette (zucchini) flesh. Toss in more of the dressing, adjust the seasoning to taste and fill the courgette (zucchini) shells with the mixture.

PER PORTION	
Kcal	130
Kjoules	520
Protein	2g
Tot. fat	11g
Sat. fat	2g
MUFA	8g
PUFA	1g
Carb.	4g
of which tot. sugar	4g
Fibre	1g

Beansprout Salad

SERVES FOUR

PREPARATION TIME: 15 MINUTES

2 × 432g (14 oz/2¼ cups) can of chickpeas (garbanzo beans), drained (*check the label for sugar*)
250g (8 oz/2½ cups) beansprouts
a large handful of fresh parsley, basil, mint, dill or chives, chopped
juice of 1 lemon
4 tablespoons olive or vegetable oil
sea salt and freshly ground black pepper

Optional Extras:

Add any of the following for a more substantial salad (*check ingredients for your allergenic food*):
250g (8 oz/1⅓ cups) canned tuna fish, sardines or pressed cod's roe
cooked chicken
chopped cooked sausage or diced garlic sausage or salami
8 rashers of bacon, fried until crisp and then diced
125g (4 oz/1 cup) well-flavoured cheese, diced

PER PORTION	
Kcal	470
Kjoules	1980
Protein	32g
Tot. fat	22g
Sat. fat	3g
MUFA	12g
PUFA	5g
Carb.	38g
of which tot. sugar	3g
Fibre	4g

Mix the chickpeas (garbanzo beans), beansprouts and chopped herbs together in a bowl. If you are using any of the extras add them at the same time.

Mix the lemon juice with the oil, season to taste with salt and pepper and stir it into the salad. Toss well and serve with lots of brown bread, if you can eat it, or a green salad.

Spinach and Mint Salad with Avocado * dairy free if yoghurt is omitted

GLUTEN, WHEAT AND EGG FREE; NO ADDED SUGAR

SERVES FOUR

PREPARATION
TIME:
15 MINUTES
+ STANDING
TIME IF DRIED
MINT IS USED

125 ml (4 fl oz/⅔ cup) yoghurt or silken tofu
juice of 1 lemon or lime
a handful of fresh mint or 1 teaspoon dried
250g (8 oz/4 cups) fresh young leaf spinach
1 small raw beetroot (beet), grated coarsely
125g (4 oz/1 cup) mushrooms, sliced thinly
1 small courgette (zucchini), sliced very thinly
1 avocado, peeled, stoned (pitted) and diced
sea salt and freshly ground black pepper

Make a dressing by putting the yoghurt or tofu in a bowl and stirring in the lemon or lime juice and salt and pepper to taste. If you are using fresh mint chop half of it finely and mix it into the dressing; if you are using dried mint, add it all to the dressing and leave it for 30 minutes to give the flavour time to develop.

To make the salad, chop most of the remaining fresh mint roughly and put it in a bowl with the spinach, beetroot (beet), mushrooms and courgette (zucchini). Arrange the diced avocado on top.

Spoon the dressing over the salad, garnish with the remaining mint and serve immediately.

PER PORTION	
Kcal	90
Kjoules	390
Protein	5g
Tot. fat	6g
Sat. fat	1g
MUFA	3g
PUFA	1g
Carb.	5g
of which tot. sugar	5g
Fibre	3g

Victorian Salad of Warm Spring Vegetables

DAIRY, GLUTEN, WHEAT AND EGG FREE; NO ADDED SUGAR

SERVES FOUR

PREPARATION AND COOKING TIME: 30 MINUTES

375g (12 oz/2½ cups) new potatoes
250g (8 oz/1⅔ cups) young carrots
16 canned artichoke hearts, sliced
2 tablespoons chopped fresh herbs, such as chives, thyme or parsley
4–6 tablespoons French dressing (see page 10)

Boil or steam the potatoes and carrots until they are just cooked, then slice them.
Arrange the sliced artichoke hearts in a wide, shallow dish. Cover them with the potato slices, then the carrots.
Just before serving, mix most of the fresh herbs into the dressing and drizzle it over the salad. Garnish with the remaining fresh herbs and serve warm.

PER PORTION	
Kcal	210
Kjoules	870
Protein	3g
Tot. fat	14g
Sat. fat	2g
MUFA	9g
PUFA	2g
Carb.	19g
of which tot. sugar	4g
Fibre	3g

Runner Bean and Avocado Salad

DAIRY, GLUTEN, WHEAT AND EGG FREE; NO ADDED SUGAR

SERVES FOUR

PREPARATION
TIME:
10 MINUTES

1 tablespoon wine vinegar
4 tablespoons olive or vegetable oil
250g (8 oz/2 cups) runner beans, sliced finely
250g (8 oz/2 cups) young courgettes (zucchini), grated coarsely
1 large avocado, peeled, stoned (pitted) and diced finely
50g (2 oz/½ cup) pumpkin seeds
2 teaspoons chopped fresh coriander (cilantro), parsley or chives
sea salt and freshly ground black pepper

Mix the vinegar and oil together with some seasoning to make a dressing.
Put all the remaining ingredients in a bowl, toss in the dressing and serve at once.

PER PORTION	
Kcal	290
Kjoules	1200
Protein	6g
Tot. fat	27g
Sat. fat	3g
MUFA	14g
PUFA	3g
Carb.	6g
of which tot. sugar	3g
Fibre	2g

Carrots in Orange Sauce
* dairy free if cream is omitted

GLUTEN, WHEAT AND EGG FREE; NO ADDED SUGAR

SERVES FOUR

PREPARATION
AND COOKING
TIME:
30 MINUTES

500g (1 lb/3¼ cups) carrots, sliced thinly
20g (¾ oz/⅛ cup) dairy-free margarine
15g (½ oz/⅒ cup) cornflour (cornstarch)
a handful of fresh parsley, chopped coarsely
125 ml (4 fl oz/⅔ cup) orange juice
2 tablespoons cream (*optional*)
sea salt and freshly ground black pepper

Cook the carrots in boiling salted water to cover for 15–20 minutes, until tender. Meanwhile, mix together the margarine, cornflour (cornstarch), parsley, orange juice and cream (if used).

Drain the carrots, reserving 200 ml (7 fl oz/ 1¼ cups) of their cooking water. Add this liquid to the creamed mixture, stirring well until it is smooth.

Add the carrots and then return the mixture to the saucepan. Cook for 2 minutes to thicken the sauce, then adjust the seasoning to taste and serve at once.

PER PORTION	
Kcal	120
Kjoules	510
Protein	2g
Tot. fat	6g
Sat. fat	2g
MUFA	2g
PUFA	1g
Carb.	17g
of which tot. sugar	13g
Fibre	4g

Stir-Fried Brussels Sprouts

DAIRY, GLUTEN, WHEAT AND EGG FREE; NO ADDED SUGAR

SERVES FOUR

PREPARATION
AND COOKING
TIME:
10 MINUTES

2 tablespoons vegetable oil

2 large garlic cloves, crushed

25g (1 oz/¼ cup) fresh ginger root, peeled and cut into tiny matchsticks

375g (12 oz/4 cups) Brussels sprouts, sliced quite finely

gluten and wheat-free soy sauce, to taste (*check the label for sugar*)

Heat the oil in a pan and lightly fry the garlic and ginger for 3 minutes.

Add the Brussels sprouts and cook, stirring constantly, over a fairly high heat for 2–3 minutes or until the sprouts are just beginning to soften. Season with soy sauce and serve at once.

PER PORTION	
Kcal	110
Kjoules	460
Protein	3g
Tot. fat	9g
Sat. fat	1g
MUFA	3g
PUFA	4g
Carb.	5g
of which tot. sugar	3g
Fibre	4g

Peperonata

SERVES FOUR

**PREPARATION
AND COOKING
TIME:
1¾ HOURS**

3 tablespoons olive oil
175g (6 oz/1½ cups) onions, chopped roughly
3 large garlic cloves, chopped finely
500g (1 lb/4 cups) red and green or red and
yellow peppers, sliced thickly
sea salt and freshly ground black pepper

Heat the oil in a heavy-based pan and gently
cook the onions and garlic until softened.
Add the peppers, stir well and cook gently for
30 minutes, stirring now and then.
Season lightly with salt and pepper and
continue to cook until the peppers are
completely soft; this can take over an hour.
Adjust the seasoning to taste and allow to cool
to room temperature before serving.

PER PORTION	
Kcal	160
Kjoules	650
Protein	2g
Tot. fat	12g
Sat. fat	2g
MUFA	8g
PUFA	2g
Carb.	12g
of which tot. sugar	10g
Fibre	3g

Cauliflower Crumble Salad
* gluten free if barley is omitted

DAIRY, EGG AND WHEAT FREE; NO ADDED SUGAR

SERVES FOUR

PREPARATION AND COOKING TIME: 30 MINUTES

200g (7 oz/1¾ cups) cauliflower
200g (7 oz/1¾ cups) broccoli
25g (1 oz/⅕ cup) pine (pignolia) kernels, cashew nuts or other nuts
juice of 1 lemon
2 tablespoons olive oil
freshly grated nutmeg
50g (2 oz/⅓ cup) pot barley or brown rice (*optional*)
100g (3½ oz/⅔ cup) can of tuna fish or 100g (3½ oz/⅔ cup) can of smoked mussels (*optional*)
sea salt and freshly ground black pepper
green salad leaves to serve

Grate the cauliflower and broccoli on a hand grater so that they look like breadcrumbs. Mix the cauliflower and broccoli with the nuts, stir in the lemon juice and oil, then season to taste with nutmeg, salt and pepper. If you want to bulk the salad up, cook the pot barley or rice in boiling salted water for 10–15 minutes or until just tender, then add it to the salad with the tuna or mussels, if used. Serve on a bed of green salad.

PER PORTION	
Kcal	170
Kjoules	730
Protein	7g
Tot. fat	13g
Sat. fat	2g
MUFA	7g
PUFA	4g
Carb.	8g
of which tot. sugar	2g
Fibre	2g

Bean and Ginger Salad

SERVES FOUR

PREPARATION
AND COOKING
TIME:
20 MINUTES

3 tablespoons olive oil
25g (1 oz/¼ cup) fresh ginger root, peeled and
chopped very finely
1 large garlic clove, chopped finely
175g (6 oz/2 cups) French beans, sliced
439g (14 oz/2 cups) can of butter (lima) beans,
drained (*check the label for sugar*)
a handful of fresh herbs, such as thyme, marjoram,
parsley or savoury, chopped, or 1 heaped
teaspoon dried mixed herbs
125 ml (4 fl oz/⅔ cup) white wine or vegetable
stock (bouillon) (*see page 2*)
sea salt and freshly ground black pepper
chopped chives, to garnish

PER PORTION	
Kcal	220
Kjoules	910
Protein	7g
Tot. fat	12g
Sat. fat	2g
MUFA	8g
PUFA	2g
Carb.	16g
of which tot. sugar	3g
Fibre	2g

Heat the olive oil in a heavy pan and add the
ginger root and garlic. Cook gently for about
5 minutes until softened, then add the French
beans and cook for 3 minutes longer.
Stir in the drained butter (lima) beans, plus
the herbs, white wine or stock (bouillon) and
season to taste.
Cook for 5 minutes until the butter (lima)
beans are thoroughly heated through, and
then adjust the seasoning, if necessary.
Serve the salad hot, warm or cold, garnished
with chopped chives.

Celery with Green Beans

DAIRY, GLUTEN, WHEAT AND EGG FREE; NO ADDED SUGAR

SERVES FOUR

PREPARATION AND COOKING TIME: 30 MINUTES

2 tablespoons vegetable oil
2 small heads of celery, chopped roughly
125g (4 oz/1⅓ cups) green beans, chopped roughly
2 bunches of spring onions (scallions), chopped finely
175 ml (6 fl oz/⅔ cup) white wine or vegetable stock (bouillon) (see *page 2*)
sea salt and freshly ground black pepper

Heat the oil in a pan and gently cook the celery for 5 minutes.
Add the green beans, spring onions (scallions), wine or stock (bouillon) and a little seasoning. Cover and simmer for 10–15 minutes or until the vegetables are tender.
Adjust the seasoning to taste and serve at once.

PER PORTION	
Kcal	120
Kjoules	490
Protein	2g
Tot. fat	8g
Sat. fat	1g
MUFA	3g
PUFA	4g
Carb.	3g
of which tot. sugar	3g
Fibre	3g

Beetroot (Beet) with Leeks
* no added sugar if honey is omitted

SERVES FOUR

PREPARATION
AND COOKING
TIME:
40 MINUTES

750g (1½ lb/4 cups) fresh young beetroot (beet),
sliced thickly
300g (10 oz/2½ cups) leeks, sliced thickly
½ teaspoon ground cumin
½ teaspoon ground coriander
400 ml (14 fl oz/1½ cups) sweet white wine, or
medium dry white wine plus 1 teaspoon honey
sea salt and freshly ground black pepper

Put the beetroot (beet), leeks and spices in
a heavy-based pan. Add the wine or wine and
honey, bring to the boil and simmer for 30
minutes or until the beetroot (beet) is tender.
Season to taste and serve either hot or cold.

PER PORTION	
Kcal	160
Kjoules	670
Protein	5g
Tot. fat	1g
Sat. fat	neg
MUFA	neg
PUFA	neg
Carb.	20g
of which tot. sugar	18g
Fibre	7g

Jerusalem Artichoke and Brussels Sprout Purée

SERVES FOUR

PREPARATION
AND COOKING
TIME:
30 MINUTES

750g (1½ lb/4 cups) Jerusalem artichokes
750g (1½ lb/4 cups) Brussels sprouts
25g (1 oz/⅕ cup) dairy-free margarine
freshly grated nutmeg
50g (2 oz/⅔ cup) sunflower seeds
sea salt and freshly ground black pepper

Steam, boil or microwave the Jerusalem artichokes and Brussels sprouts until they are tender. Preheat the grill (broiler).
Drain both vegetables and purée them in a food processor or liquidiser with the margarine and nutmeg, salt and pepper to taste.
Stir half the sunflower seeds into the purée and sprinkle the rest over the top.
Toast lightly under the grill (broiler) and serve at once.

PER PORTION	
Kcal	310
Kjoules	1360
Protein	13g
Tot. fat	17g
Sat. fat	3g
MUFA	4g
PUFA	8g
Carb.	31g
of which tot. sugar	9g
Fibre	7g

Desserts

So many desserts seem to rely on cream, cake or sugar as their main constituents that you can feel distinctly deprived if you are not allowed to enjoy them. However, it is amazing what fruit sugar and a little ingenuity can achieve without a drop of cream or a spoonful of flour.

Christmas Pudding

DAIRY, GLUTEN, WHEAT AND EGG FREE; NO ADDED SUGAR

SERVES EIGHT

PREPARATION
AND COOKING
TIME:
2 HOURS +
1½ HOURS IF
REHEATING

40g (1½ oz/¼ cup) fructose or 50g (2 oz/⅓ cup) pale muscovado (brown) sugar
50g (2 oz/⅓ cup) soya flour
150g (5 oz/1 cup) brown ground rice
7g sachet of easy blend (instant) yeast
½ teaspoon gluten and wheat-free mixed (pie) spice
½ teaspoon cinnamon
½ teaspoon nutmeg
300 ml (½ pint/1⅓ cups) orange juice
50g (2 oz/⅓ cup) soft dairy-free margarine
1 small eating apple
375g (12 oz/⅓ cup) dried mixed fruit
grated zest of 1 lemon
grated zest of 1 orange

PER PORTION	
Kcal	310
Kjoules	1320
Protein	5g
Tot. fat	7g
MUFA	2g
PUFA	2g
Carb.	60g
of which tot. sugar	44g
Fibre	4g

Mix the fructose or sugar, soya flour, ground rice, yeast and spices well together.
Add the orange juice and margarine and grate in the apple. Beat until smooth, then add the dried fruit and grated lemon and orange zest and mix well.
Grease a 1.5 litre (2½-pint) pudding basin and spoon in the mixture. Tie on a double greaseproof lid and make a string handle. Lower the basin into a large saucepan one-third full of water, cover tightly and steam for at least 1½ hours.
Like all Christmas puddings, this pudding stores well; reheat before serving by steaming for 1½ hours.

Top: Potato, Leek and Apple Pie, page 61

Bottom: Baked Fennel with Spinach and Root Vegetables, page 58

Mushroom and
Sunflower Seed
Flan, page 62

Beetroot (Beet)
Artichoke and
Ginger Stir-fry,
page 64

Rice, Chilli and
Bamboo Shoot
Casserole,
page 65

Chickpeas (Garbanzo
Beans) with Chillies
and Peppers, page 66

Okra and
Potato Stew,
page 70

Mixed Vegetables
with Carrot and
Onion Purée,
page 71

Spinach and
Mint Salad
with Avocado,
page 79

Victorian Salad of Warm
Spring Vegetables, page 80

Top: Cauliflower Crumble Salad, page 85

Bottom: Bean and Ginger Salad, page 86

Gooey Chocolate
Mousse,
page 96

Apple Flan, page 97

Fruit Cake,
page 106

Flapjacks,
page 103

No-Butter Brandy Butter

SERVES EIGHT

PREPARATION TIME:
5 MINUTES

125g (4 oz/⅔ cup) dairy-free margarine
75g (3 oz/½ cup) fructose or 125g (4 oz/⅔ cup) pale muscovado (brown) sugar
2–4 tablespoons brandy

Beat the margarine and fructose or sugar together until very light and fluffy (this can be done in a food processor or with an electric mixer).
Gradually add brandy to taste, continuing to beat hard.

PER PORTION	
Kcal	180
Kjoules	750
Protein	neg
Tot. fat	13g
Sat. fat	4g
MUFA	5g
PUFA	3g
Carb.	13g
of which tot. sugar	13g
Fibre	–

Chocolate Profiteroles

SERVES SIX

PREPARATION
AND COOKING
TIME:
1 HOUR

For the Profiteroles:
250 ml (8 fl oz/1 cup) water
75g (3 oz/½ cup) dairy-free margarine
125g (4 oz/1 cup) plain white flour, sifted
3 eggs, beaten
cocoa powder, for dusting

For the Filling:
25g (1 oz/¼ cup) cocoa powder
15g (½ oz/⅒ cup) cornflour (cornstarch)
300 ml (½ pint/1⅓ cups) soya milk
75g (3 oz/½ cup) dairy-free dark chocolate
50g (2 oz/¼ cup) raw cane sugar
1 tablespoon brandy or water
250g (8 oz/2 cups) silken tofu, puréed

For the Sauce:
250g (8 oz/1⅓ cups) dairy-free dark chocolate
125–150 ml (4–5 fl oz/⅔ cup) water
2 tablespoons brandy (*optional*)

PER PORTION	
Kcal	600
Kjoules	2500
Protein	13g
Tot. fat	33g
Sat. fat	14g
MUFA	11g
PUFA	5g
Carb.	64g
of which tot. sugar	42g
Fibre	1g

Preheat the oven to Gas Mark 7/220°C/425°F.
Put the water and margarine in a pan and
bring to the boil.
Tip all the flour at once into the liquid and
then beat thoroughly until the mixture is
smooth and comes away from the sides of the
pan.

Add the eggs gradually, beating all the time, until the dough is smooth and shiny.

Spoon walnut-size dollops of the dough on to some foil or greaseproof paper laid out on a baking sheet and bake for 15–20 minutes, until lightly browned and firm to the touch.

Remove the profiteroles from the oven and, as soon as they are cool enough to handle, split them open and remove any uncooked dough from the inside; leave to cool.

For the filling, put the cocoa and cornflour (cornstarch) in a pan and, over a gentle heat, gradually add the soya milk, stirring until the mixture is smooth.

Break up the chocolate, add it to the pan with the sugar and cook until both are melted.

Stir in the brandy or water and then leave to cool.

When the mixture is almost cold, stir in the tofu. Fill the profiteroles shortly before serving.

For the sauce, melt the chocolate with the water over a very gentle heat. When it is quite smooth, add the brandy, if used.

Dust the filled profiteroles with cocoa powder and pour over the hot sauce just before serving.

Gooey Chocolate Mousse

DAIRY, GLUTEN AND WHEAT FREE

SERVES FOUR

PREPARATION TIME:

30 MINUTES

175g (6 oz/1 cup) dairy-free dark chocolate
4 tablespoons silken tofu
3 eggs, separated
2 tablespoons brandy
40g (1½ oz/¼ cup) preserved stem ginger, chopped finely
25g (1 oz/¼ cup) pistachio nuts, chopped cocoa powder, for dusting

Melt the chocolate in a bowl set over a pan of very hot water or in a microwave.

Purée the tofu with the egg yolks and stir this mixture thoroughly into the chocolate – you may need to keep the bowl over hot water to prevent the chocolate cooling and becoming unmanageable.

Add the brandy, stem ginger and pistachio nuts (reserving a few to sprinkle over the top) and mix thoroughly.

Whisk the egg whites until they hold their shape in soft peaks. Stir a third of the egg whites into the chocolate mixture to lighten it, then gently but thoroughly fold in the remainder.

Pour the mixture into four glasses or ramekin dishes, dust with cocoa powder and sprinkle over the reserved chopped pistachios. Chill until ready to serve.

PER PORTION	
Kcal	380
Kjoules	1600
Protein	10g
Tot. fat	21g
Sat. fat	9g
MUFA	6g
PUFA	1g
Carb.	35g
of which tot. sugar	28g
Fibre	8g

Apple Flan
* gluten free if gluten-free pastry is used

SERVES FOUR

PREPARATION
AND COOKING
TIME:
I HOUR

20-cm (8-inch) pastry case (shell) made from
oat pastry (see *page 107*) or gluten-free pastry
(page 108)
3 large Bramley cooking apples, peeled, cored and
chopped roughly
6 tablespoons silken tofu
1 heaped teaspoon cornflour (cornstarch)
juice of 2 large oranges
juice of 1 large lemon

Preheat the oven to Gas Mark 4/180°C/350°F.
Line the pastry case (shell) with foil or greaseproof paper, weight it with beans or rice and
bake blind (empty) for about 20 minutes. Take
it out of the oven, remove the paper and beans
or rice and set aside.
Reduce the oven temperature to Gas Mark 3/
160°/325°F.
Put the apples in the flan case.
Liquidise the tofu with the cornflour
(cornstarch) and the orange and lemon juice
and pour it over the apples (if it is too thick to
pour, add a little more orange juice). Bake for
20 minutes or until the apples are just cooked
but still slightly crunchy and the top of the pie
is lightly browned. Serve warm or cold.

PER PORTION	
Kcal	570
Kjoules	2380
Protein	17g
Tot. fat	36g
Sat. fat	9g
MUFA	12g
PUFA	9g
Carb.	48g
of which tot. sugar	18g
Fibre	7g

Apple Soufflé

SERVES
FOUR–SIX

PREPARATION
AND COOKING
TIME:
45 MINUTES

500g (1 lb/4 cups) Bramley apples, peeled, cored and chopped
2 tablespoons fructose, apple or pear concentrate or muscovado sugar
1 tablespoon cornflour (cornstarch)
5 tablespoons Calvados or other brandy or liqueur
3 eggs plus 1 egg white

Preheat the oven to Gas Mark 5/190°C/375°F. Put the apples in a pan with the sweetener and 2 tablespoons of water and cook gently for 10–15 minutes until completely soft. Beat with a wooden spoon to make a purée.

Blend the cornflour (cornstarch) with a little of the apple purée then add it to the pan and cook gently for a few minutes until it thickens slightly. Remove from the heat and stir in the alcohol.

Separate the eggs and stir the yolks into the apple mixture.

Whisk the egg whites until they form soft peaks. Stir a third of the whites into the apple mixture, then gently fold in the rest. Spoon the mixture into a 1.2 litre (2-pint) soufflé dish or 4–6 individual ramekin dishes and bake for 15–20 minutes if using a soufflé dish or 10–15 minutes for ramekin dishes, until risen and lightly browned. Serve at once.

PER PORTION	
Kcal	180
Kjoules	770
Protein	6g
Tot. fat	4g
Sat. fat	1g
MUFA	2g
PUFA	1g
Carb.	21g
of which tot. sugar	9g
Fibre	3g

Summer Fruit and Nut Crisp

* gluten and wheat free if flour is omitted;
no added sugar if fructose is omitted

DAIRY AND EGG FREE

SERVES FOUR

PREPARATION
AND COOKING
TIME:
45 MINUTES

1kg (2 lb/6½ cups) mixed soft summer fruits, such as raspberries, strawberries, loganberries, currants, bilberries, etc.
fructose or apple or pear concentrate, to taste
75g (3 oz/1 cup) hazelnuts and 75g (3 oz/1 cup) flaked almonds, toasted, or use 75g (3 oz/1 cup) either nut, toasted and mixed with 75g (3 oz/ ⅔ cup) wholemeal flour

Preheat the oven to Gas Mark 4/180°C/350°F. Put the fruit in a saucepan containing about 2.5 cm (1 inch) of water and cook gently for a few minutes until the juices run. Sweeten to taste with the fructose or fruit concentrate. Drain off the excess juice and reserve.
Chop the nuts roughly in a food processor, then stir in the flour, if used. Spoon the fruit into an ovenproof dish and cover with the nuts. Bake for 20–30 minutes or until slightly crunchy and browned.
Serve with soya cream or yoghurt, if you can eat it, and the warmed fruit juices.

PER PORTION	
Kcal	330
Kjoules	1390
Protein	10g
Tot. fat	23g
Sat. fat	2g
MUFA	16g
PUFA	4g
Carb.	23g
of which tot. sugar	22g
Fibre	17g

Soya Milk Shake

SERVES ONE

PREPARATION TIME:

5 MINUTES

125g (4 oz/¾ cup) fresh fruit, such as strawberries or banana, chopped

4 tablespoons plain or fruit soya yoghurt

1 tablespoon apple or pear concentrate

4 tablespoons vanilla or fruit soya ice cream

Purée the fresh fruit, yoghurt and fruit concentrate in a liquidiser until smooth. Add the ice cream and purée again. Taste and add more concentrate if necessary. Serve at once.

PER PORTION	
Kcal	170
Kjoules	700
Protein	7g
Tot. fat	5g
Sat. fat	1g
MUFA	1g
PUFA	3g
Carb.	25g
of which tot. sugar	24g
Fibre	3g

Baking

Baking is the area where the coeliac and those who are wheat
intolerant suffer most. Although you can never make 'real' bread
without wheat and gluten, there are some excellent alternatives and
some delicious gluten-free cakes and biscuits that will have every
member of the family asking for more.

Chocolate Cake
* dairy free if butter is omitted

MAKES A 20CM (8-INCH) ROUND CAKE

PREPARATION AND COOKING TIME: 1 HOUR

75g (3 oz/½ cup) butter or dairy-free margarine
250g (8 oz/1¼ cups) dark muscovado sugar
6 tablespoons boiling water
4 tablespoons gluten and wheat-free cocoa powder
3 eggs
125g (4 oz/⅔ cup) ground rice or rice flour
1 teaspoon gluten and wheat-free baking powder
75g (3 oz/1 cup) ground almonds

Preheat the oven to Gas Mark 4/180°C/350°F. Beat together the butter or margarine and sugar until light and fluffy.

Pour the boiling water over the cocoa powder and mix well, then beat it into the creamed mixture. Beat in the eggs one at a time, adding a spoonful of ground rice or rice flour with each egg.

Mix together the baking powder, ground almonds and the remaining rice and fold into the mixture. Spoon it into a 20-cm (8-inch) cake tin lined with greaseproof paper and bake for about 35 minutes or until the cake is firm to the touch. Turn the cake out on to a wire rack and leave to cool.

PER PORTION	
Kcal	2740
Kjoules	11,480
Protein	48g
Tot. fat	125g
Sat. fat	51g
MUFA	49g
PUFA	15g
Carb.	370g
of which tot. sugar	264g
Fibre	10g

Flapjacks

MAKES
EIGHT–TEN

PREPARATION
AND COOKING
TIME:
30 MINUTES

250g (8 oz/2⅔ cups) porridge oats
125g (4 oz/¾ cup) dairy-free margarine
125g (4 fl oz/½ cup) apple or pear concentrate
50g (2 oz/⅔ cup) pine (pignolia) kernels or
sunflower seeds

Preheat the oven to Gas Mark 2/150°C/300°F.
Lightly process the oats in a food processor.
Melt the margarine in a pan with the fruit
concentrate. Stir in the oats and pine
(pignolia) kernels or sunflower seeds and
mix well.

Press the mixture into an 18-cm (7-inch)
square tin. Bake for 20 minutes or until lightly
browned, then remove from the oven and
mark into 8 or 10 pieces with a knife. When
the flapjacks are cold, remove them carefully
from the tin.

TOTAL QUANTITY	
Kcal	2340
Kjoules	9900
Protein	45g
Tot. fat	144g
Sat. fat	36g
MUFA	54g
PUFA	54g
Carb.	234g
of which tot. sugar	45g
Fibre	18g

Lemon or Orange Cake

MAKES A 500G
(1 LB) CAKE

PREPARATION
AND COOKING
TIME:
1 HOUR

125g (4 oz/¾ cup) dairy-free margarine
125g (4 oz/⅔ cup) raw cane muscovado sugar or
75g (3 oz/½ cup) fructose
grated zest and juice of 2 lemons or 2 small
oranges
125 ml (4 fl oz/½ cup) silken tofu, puréed in a
food processor
175g (6 oz/1¼ cups) self-raising flour, wholemeal,
white or half and half
2 level teaspoons baking powder

Preheat the oven to Gas Mark 3/160°C/325°F.
Cream together the margarine and sugar or
fructose until light. Beat in the lemon or
orange zest and juice and the tofu, then fold
in the flour and baking powder.
Spoon the mixture into a greased and lined
500g (1 lb) loaf tin (pan), mounding it slightly
in the middle, and bake for 40 minutes. Turn
out of the tin and cool on a wire rack.

PER CAKE	
Kcal	2120
Kjoules	8890
Protein	30g
Tot. fat	110g
Sat. fat	32g
MUFA	40g
PUFA	31g
Carb.	269g
of which tot. sugar	146g
Fibre	11g

Gingerbread

MAKES A 2KG
(2LB) LOAF
OR A 20CM
(8-INCH)
ROUND CAKE

PREPARATION
AND COOKING
TIME:
I HOUR

125g (4 oz/¾ cup) dairy-free margarine
125g (4 oz/⅔ cup) raw cane demerara sugar or dark muscovado sugar
375g (12 oz/1 cup) black treacle (molasses)
250g (8 oz/2⅔ cups) porridge oats
4 eggs
1 heaped teaspoon baking powder
2 teaspoons ground ginger
1 heaped teaspoon mixed (pie) spice
1 heaped teaspoon ground cinnamon

Preheat the oven to Gas Mark 3/160°C325°F. Melt the margarine, sugar and treacle (molasses) together in a pan and then remove from the heat.

Process the oats to a powder in a food processor.

Beat the eggs into the melted mixture followed by the oats, baking powder and spices. Pour into a greased 1kg (2 lb) loaf tin (pan) or a deep 20 cm (8-inch) round cake tin and bake for 45 minutes or until a skewer inserted in the centre comes out clean. Remove from the oven, turn out of the tin and leave to cool on a wire rack.

PER PORTION	
Kcal	3700
Kjoules	15,570
Protein	62g
Tot. fat	146g
Sat. fat	41g
MUFA	56g
PUFA	39g
Carb.	571g
of which tot. sugar	385g
Fibre	16g

Fruit Cake

**MAKES AN
18CM (7-INCH)
SQUARE OR
20CM (8-INCH)
ROUND CAKE**

**PREPARATION
AND COOKING
TIME:
2 HOURS**

250g (8 oz/1⅔ cups) dairy-free vegetable margarine
150g (5 oz/¾ cup) raw cane muscovado sugar or 100g (3½ oz/½ cup) fructose
grated zest and juice of 2 oranges
grated zest and juice of ½ lemon
4 tablespoons silken tofu, creamed
250g (8 oz/⅔ cup) self-raising flour, wholemeal, white or half and half
3 level teaspoons baking powder
50g (2 oz/⅔ cup) ground almonds
50g (2 oz/⅔ cup) flaked almonds
125g (4 oz/¾ cup) sultanas
125g (4 oz/¾ cup) raisins

PER PORTION	
Kcal	4680
Kjoules	19,530
Protein	63g
Tot. fat	270g
Sat. fat	72g
MUFA	117g
PUFA	72g
Carb.	540g
of which tot. sugar	360g
Fibre	45g

Preheat the oven to Gas Mark 2/150°C/300°F. Cream the margarine and sugar together until light and fluffy. Beat in the orange and lemon zest and juice, then beat in the tofu along with 4 tablespoons of the flour mixed with the baking powder. Carefully fold in the rest of the flour with the ground almonds, flaked almonds and dried fruit. If the mixture is too dry, add a little more orange juice.

Grease an 18 cm (7-inch) square or a 20 cm (8-inch) round tin and spoon in the mixture, mounding it slightly in the middle as without eggs the cake will sink a little as it cooks.

Bake for 1½ hours. Remove the cake from the oven, cool slightly in the tin, then turn out on to a wire rack to cool completely.

Oat Pastry

MAKES ENOUGH TO LINE A 20CM (8-INCH) FLAN TIN

PREPARATION TIME: 10 MINUTES

250g (8 oz/2⅔ cups) porridge oats

150g (5 oz/1 cup) dairy-free margarine

Process the oats to a powder in a food processor, then rub in the margarine until well combined.

Press the pastry over the base and sides of a 20 cm (8-inch) flan tin and then use as directed in the recipe. The oats make a very crumbly but delicious pastry.

TOTAL QUANTITY	
Kcal	2080
Kjoules	8800
Protein	32g
Tot. fat	144g
Sat. fat	40g
MUFA	56g
PUFA	40g
Carb.	184g
of which tot. sugar	neg
Fibre	16g

Gluten-free Pastry
* egg free if egg is omitted

**MAKES
ENOUGH TO
LINE A
20–23CM
(8–9 INCH)
FLAN TIN**

125g (4 oz/¾ cup) brown rice flour
125g (4 oz/¾ cup) soya flour
½ teaspoon gluten-free baking powder
125g (4 oz/¾ cup) dairy-free margarine
2 tablespoons water or 1 egg

**PREPARATION
TIME:
10 MINUTES**

Mix the brown rice flour and soya flour with the baking powder. Rub in the margarine and stir in the water or egg to make a soft dough. Press on to the base and sides of a 20–23 cm (8–9 inch) flan tin and then use as directed in the recipe.

This pastry will be too crumbly to turn out of the tin.

TOTAL QUANTITY	
Kcal	1980
Kjoules	8220
Protein	60g
Tot. fat	138g
Sat. fat	36g
MUFA	48g
PUFA	36g
Carb.	132g
of which tot. sugar	18g
Fibre	18g

Oat Bread

MAKES 2 X
500G (1 LB)
LOAVES

PREPARATION
AND COOKING
TIME:
1 HOUR 20
MINUTES +
RISING

500g (1 lb/5⅓ cups) porridge oats
7g sachet of easy blend (instant) yeast
1½ teaspoons salt
1 tablespoon raw cane sugar or 1 dessertspoon fructose
400 ml (14 fl oz/1½ cups) warm water
1 tablespoon vegetable oil

Preheat the oven to Gas Mark 4/180°C/350°F.
Process the oats in a food processor until they are the consistency of flour. Put them in a bowl with the yeast, salt and sugar or fructose, then stir in the water and oil. Beat hard by hand or in a mixer or food processor for at least 5 minutes.

Spoon the mixture into 2 well-greased 500g (1 lb) loaf tins, cover and leave in a warm place for 30 minutes, until slightly risen.
Bake for 1 hour, then turn the loaves out of the tins and leave to cool on a wire rack.

PER LOAF	
Kcal	1130
Kjoules	4780
Protein	36g
Tot. fat	30g
Sat. fat	5g
MUFA	11g
PUFA	13g
Carb.	193g
of which tot. sugar	11g
Fibre	18g

Wholemeal Brown Loaf

* dairy free if butter not used

Similar in taste and texture to a fairly dense wholemeal wheaten loaf.

GLUTEN AND WHEAT FREE

MAKES ONE	350g (12½ oz/2½ cups) brown rice flour
1 LB LOAF	50g (1¾ oz/⅓ cup) buckwheat flour
	50g (1¾ oz/⅓ cup) potato flour
PREPARATION	1 teaspoon soya flour
AND COOKING	½ teaspoon salt
TIME:	2 teaspoons sugar
40 MINUTES	1½ teaspoons cream of tartar
	¼ teaspoon bicarbonate of soda (baking soda)
	2 teaspoon easy bake (instant) yeast
	20g (¾ oz) butter or dairy-free spread
	1 medium egg
	425 ml warm water

PER LOAF	
Kcal	150
Kjoules	610
Protein	2g
Tot. fat	8g
Sat. fat	1g
MUFA	5g
PUFA	1g
Carb.	6g
of which tot. sugar	4g
Fibre	2g

Heat the oven to Gas Mark 4/180°C/350°F.
Grease a loaf tin (pan) or a round cake tin.
Mix all the dry ingredients except the sesame
seeds thoroughly in a large mixing bowl. Rub
in the butter, then stir in the egg and half the
sesame seeds, if you are using them. Make up
the 425 ml of warm water with 150 ml of
boiling water, cooled with 275 ml of tap water.
Stir this gradually into the dry mix. This will
make an extremely runny mixture, but do not
worry as it will firm up in the baking.
Warm the tin and then pour in the mixture.
Sprinkle over the remaining sesame seeds and
bake it in the centre of the oven for 40
minutes or until it is risen and a skewer comes
out clean.

Cool in the tin for 5–10 minutes under a teacloth then carefully knock out onto the rack. Cover with a teacloth and leave until it is quite cold before cutting.

Banana Bread
* dairy free if dairy-free spread and soya or coconut milk used

GLUTEN AND WHEAT FREE; NO ADDED SUGAR

PREPARATION
AND COOKING
TIME:
1–1½ HOURS

100g (3½ oz/⅔ cup) butter or dairy-free spread
50 ml (2 fl oz/¼ cup) cow, sheep, goat, soya or coconut milk
225g (8 oz/1½ cups) gram or chickpea (garbanzo bean) flour, sifted
2 medium eggs
1 level teaspoon bicarbonate of soda (baking soda)
3 large, very ripe bananas

Preheat the oven to Gas Mark 4/170°C/350°F. Beat the spread with the eggs and milk until they are pale and fluffy.
Sift the flour with the bicarbonate and add it alternately with the eggs.
Mash the bananas and add them to the mixture with the milk. Spoon the mixture into a loaf tin (pan) and bake in a moderate oven for 1–1½ hours or until a skewer comes out clean. Cool on a rack.

PER LOAF	
Kcal	150
Kjoules	610
Protein	2g
Tot. fat	8g
Sat. fat	1g
MUFA	5g
PUFA	1g
Carb.	6g
of which tot. sugar	4g
Fibre	2g

Almond and Rice Flour Bread

PREPARATION
AND COOKING
TIME:
40 MINUTES

150g (5⅓ oz/1¾ cups) ground almonds
30g (1 oz/¼ cup) buckwheat flour
20g (¾ oz/½ cup) rice flour
3 heaped teaspoons wheat and gluten-free baking powder
pinch salt
2 tablespoons olive oil
175 ml (6 oz/⅔ cup) coconut milk (you can get it tinned)

Heat the oven to Gas Mark 4/180°C/350°F. Mix all the dry ingredients together thoroughly. Stir in the oil and then the milk. It will make a rather sloppy mixture but don't worry about that as the buckwheat absorbs an enormous amount of liquid. Pour the mixture into a well-oiled small loaf tin (pan) and bake for 40 minutes or until a skewer comes out clean.

Remove from the oven, cover lightly with a tea towel and allow to cool in the tin. Knock out of the tin and slice.

PER LOAF	
Kcal	150
Kjoules	610
Protein	2g
Tot. fat	8g
Sat. fat	1g
MUFA	5g
PUFA	1g
Carb.	6g
of which tot. sugar	4g
Fibre	2g

Raisin Muffins

* dairy free if dairy-free spread and soya or coconut milk used

MAKES SIX

PREPARATION AND COOKING TIME: 20 MINUTES

75g (2¾ oz/½ cup) butter or dairy-free spread
40g (1½ oz/¼ cup) light muscovado sugar
1 small egg
120 ml (3¾ fl oz/½ cup) cow, sheep, goat, soya or coconut milk
75g (2¾ oz/½ cup) sifted gram or chickpea (garbanzo bean) flour
75g (2¾ oz/½ cup) rice flour
1 heaped teaspoon wheat and gluten-free baking powder
small pinch salt
60g (2½ oz/½ cup) raisins

Heat the oven to Gas Mark 4/180°C/350°F. Beat the butter or spread, sugar, egg and milk together with an electric beater. Mix the flours with the baking powder and salt and gradually beat them into the liquid mixture. Fold in the raisins and spoon the dough into six greased mince pie or tart pans. Bake the muffins for 20 minutes or until they are risen and firm to the touch. Remove them and cool them slightly on a rack. The muffins are also good cold and freeze well.

PER PORTION	
Kcal	150
Kjoules	610
Protein	2g
Tot. fat	8g
Sat. fat	1g
MUFA	5g
PUFA	1g
Carb.	6g
of which tot. sugar	4g
Fibre	2g

Gram Flour Sponge Cake
* dairy free if dairy-free spread used

MAKES A 20CM
(8-INCH) CAKE

PREPARATION
AND COOKING
TIME:
45 MINUTES

200g (7 oz/1 cup) butter or dairy-free spread
200g (7 oz/1cup) light muscovado sugar
3 medium eggs
200g (7 oz/1½ cups) sifted gram or chickpea
(garbanzo bean) flour
2 level teaspoons gluten and wheat-free baking
powder
1 teaspoon vanilla essence

Heat the oven to Gas Mark 4/180°C/350°F.
Beat the butter or spread with the sugar until
light and fluffy. Beating slowly, add the eggs
alternatively with the flour. Fold in the
remaining flour, baking powder and vanilla
essence.

Spoon into a well-oiled or lined 20 cm
(8-inch) tin and bake it for 30 minutes or
until the cake is firm to the touch and a
skewer comes out clean. Cool on a rack and
when cold, split and fill with jam (jelly) of
your choice. If you wish you can also dust the
top with icing (confectioner's) sugar or soft
muscovado sugar.

Apple Cake
* dairy free if dairy-free spread and soya or coconut milk are used

MAKES A 20CM
(8-INCH)
SQUARE CAKE

PREPARATION
AND COOKING
TIME:
30–40 MINUTES

100g (3½ oz/½ cup) butter or dairy-free spread
200g (7 oz/1½ cups) dried dates, finely chopped
½ teaspoon ground nutmeg
1 level teaspoon ground ginger
225g (8 oz/2 cups) tart eating apples, cored, peeled and grated
130g (4½ oz/1 cup) rice flour
130g (4½ oz/1 cup) gram or chickpea (garbanzo bean) flour
2 heaped teaspoons gluten and wheat-free baking powder
100g (4 oz/¾ cup) sultanas
2 medium eggs
175 ml (6 fl oz/⅔ cup) cow, sheep, goat, soya or coconut milk

Preheat the oven to Gas Mark 4/180°C/350°F and grease and line a 20 cm (8-inch) square tin.
Put the butter or spread, dates, apple and spices into a processor and blend thoroughly. Fold in the sultanas and eggs, alternately with the flour and milk. When all are amalgamated transfer them into a 20-cm (8-inch) tin.
Bake for 30–40 minutes until dark golden and firm to the touch. Test with a skewer. Remove from the oven and leave to cool in the tin for 10–15 minutes before turning on to a wire rack to cool completely.

Coffee and Walnut Cake

DAIRY, GLUTEN AND WHEAT FREE; NO ADDED SUGAR

**MAKES 20CM
(8-INCH) CAKE**

**PREPARATION
AND COOKING
TIME:
1 HOUR**

150g (5¼ oz/¾ cup) dairy-free spread
100g (3½ oz/¾ cup) softened dried dates
50g (3½ oz/⅔ cup) softened dried figs
3 heaped teaspoons /1 tablespoon instant coffee
2 tablespoons boiling water
3 eggs
50g rice flour
100g (3½ oz/¾ cup) sifted gram or chickpea (garbanzo bean) flour
2 teaspoons wheat and gluten-free baking powder
50g (1¾ oz/½ cup) broken walnuts

PER PORTION	
Kcal	150
Kjoules	610
Protein	2g
Tot. fat	8g
Sat. fat	1g
MUFA	5g
PUFA	1g
Carb.	6g
of which tot. sugar	4g
Fibre	2g

Preheat the oven to Gas Mark 4/180°C/350°F.
In a food processor pulverise the spread with the dates and figs. When they are really well amalgamated, transfer to a bowl.
Meanwhile, melt the coffee in the water. Add the coffee to the fruit and fat mixture then stir in the eggs alternately with a spoonful of flour. Fold in the rest of the flour with the baking powder and then the walnuts.
Transfer to a well-oiled round/square cake tin (lined with greaseproof paper unless you are absolutely sure that it will not stick) and bake for 45 minutes or until a skewer comes out clean. Turn out onto a rack to cool.
The cake can be eaten as it is or iced with whatever kind of icing you are able to eat.

Gram Flour Pastry
* dairy free if dairy-free spread is used

SERVES FOUR

PREPARATION AND COOKING TIME:

45 MINUTES

125g (5 oz/1 cup) gram or chickpea (garbanzo beans) flour

60g (2 oz/¼ cup) butter or dairy-free spread

approx. 4 tablespoons water

Cut and rub the fat into the flour until it is well crumbed. Add the water and mix to a dough. It will be a bit sticky but don't worry about that. Chill for 30–60 minutes before using.

Use extra gram flour to dust a board then roll out as normal.

PER PORTION	
Kcal	150
Kjoules	610
Protein	2g
Tot. fat	8g
Sat. fat	1g
MUFA	5g
PUFA	1g
Carb.	6g
of which tot. sugar	4g
Fibre	2g

Lemon Shortbread

**MAKES APPROX.
12 BISCUITS**

**PREPARATION
AND COOKING
TIME:
30 MINUTES**

These shortbread are more crumbly than those made with wheat flour so need careful handling – but they do taste excellent.

50g (1¾ oz/¼ cup) butter
75g (2¾ oz/⅓ cup) pale muscovado sugar
50g (1¾ oz/½ cup) ground almonds
100g (3½ oz/1 cup) gram or chickpea (garbanzo bean) flour
grated rind of 1 lemon

Beat the butter with the sugar with an electric whisk until soft and light.
Add the lemon rind, then rub in the ground almonds and gram flour with your fingers, working as lightly as you can. Pat the mixture out into the bottom of a tin or shape it into a round approximately 20 cm wide and bake it in a moderate oven (Gas mark 3/160°C/ 325°F) for 15 minutes.
Remove and score the break points (it should make around 12) with a knife then return to the oven for another 5 minutes. Cool slightly then cut along the score marks, remove carefully, with a spatula, to a rack to get quite cold.

PER PORTION	
Kcal	150
Kjoules	610
Protein	2g
Tot. fat	8g
Sat. fat	1g
MUFA	5g
PUFA	1g
Carb.	6g
of which tot. sugar	4g
Fibre	2g

Useful Addresses

Please send a large stamped, self-addressed envelope to any group with your request for help.

Organizations
UK

Action Against Allergy,
24–6 High Street,
Hampton Hill,
Middlesex TW12 1PD

Allergy-Induced Autism,
3 Palmera Avenue,
Calcot,
Reading,
Berks RG3 7DZ

Anaphylaxis Campaign,
8 Wey Close,
Aldershot,
Hampshire GU12 6LY

British Diabetic Association,
10 Queen Anne Street,
London W1M 0BD

British Dietetic Association,
Elizabeth House,
Suffolk Street,
Queensway,
Birmingham B1 1LS

British Goat Society,
34–36 Fore Street,
Bovey Tracey,
Newton Abbot,
Devon TQ13 9AD

British Sheep Dairying
Association,
Wield Wood,
Alresford,
Hampshire SO24 9RU

Coeliac Society,
PO Box 220,
High Wycombe,
Buckinghamshire HP11 2HY

Food Intolerance Databank,
Leatherhead Food RA,
Randalls Road,
Leatherhead,
Surrey KT22 7RY

Hyperactive Children's Support
Group,
71 Whycke Lane,
Chichester,
West Sussex PO19 2LD

IBS Network,
Centre for Human Nutrition,
Northern General Hospital,
Sheffield S5 7AU

Institute for Optimum
Nutrition,
Blades Court,
Deodar Road,
London SW15 2NU

Midlands Asthma and Allergy
Research Association,
12 Vernon Street,
Derby DE1 1FT

Myalgic Encephalomyelitis
(ME) Association,
PO Box 87,
Stanford-le-Hope,
Essex SS17 8EX

National Eczema Society,
Tavistock House East,
Tavistock Square,
London WC1H 9SR

National Society for Research
into Allergy,
PO Box 45,
Hinckley,
Leicestershire LE10 1JY

Nutrition Associates,
Galtres House,
Lysander Close,
Clifton Moregate,
York YO3 0XB

Vegetarian Society,
Parkdale,
Dunham Road,
Altrincham,
Cheshire WA12 4QG

USA

Allergy Resources Inc.,
PO Box 888,
Palmer Lake,
CO 80133

American Allergy Association,
PO Box 7273,
Menlo Park
CA 94026

American Celiac Society,
Dietary Support Coalition,
Ms Annette Bentley,
58 Musano Court,
West Orange,
NJ 07052

Asthma and Allergy Foundation
of America,
1717 Massachusetts Avenue,
Suite 305,
Washington DC 20036

Gluten Intolerance Group,
PO Box 23053,
Seattle,
WA 98102

Stockists
UK

Allergy Care,
9 Corporation Street,
Taunton,
Somerset TA1 4AJ
Tel: 01823 325 023

D & D Specialist Chocolates,
Berrydale House,
5 Lawn Road,
London NW3 2XS
Tel: 0171 722 2866

Chocolates and seasonal novelties. Gluten, dairy, sugar or
cocoa free.

Farm-a-round
Tel: 0181 291 4519
Organic fruit and vegetables
delivered to your door.

H. R. Higgins Ltd,
79 Duke Street,
London W1M 6AS
Tel: 0171 629 3913
Specialist coffee supplier.

Wholefood Organically Grown
Produce,
24 Paddington Street,
London W1M 4DR

USA

Arrowhead Mills Inc.,
Box 2059,
Hereford,
TX 79045
Tel: 800 749 0730
Fax: 806 364 8242
Mail order suppliers of grains,
flours, pulses (legumes), cereals
and seeds.

Bob's Red Mill Natural Foods
Inc.,
5209 S. E. International Way,
Milwauke,
OR 97222
Tel: 503 654 3215
Fax: 503 653 1339
Mail order stockists of grains,
flours, pulses (legumes), cereals
and seeds.

Ener-g Foods Inc.,
PO Box 84487,
Seattle,
WA 98124–5787
Tel: 8700 331 5222
Fax: 206 764 3398
Suppliers of food allergy
products, many rice-based
including rice flours, rice pasta,
egg replacer, almond milk mix as
well as baked goods.

Gold Mine Natural Food Co.,
3419 Hancock Street,
San Diego,
CA 921110–4307
Tel: 800 475 3663
Fax: 619 296 9756
Stockist of rice, barley and other
organic grains and seeds.

Jaffe Brothers Natural Foods,
PO Box 636,
Valley Center,
CA 92082–0636
Tel: 616 749 1133
Fax: 619 749 1282
Wholefood suppliers of nuts, nut
butters, dried fruits and grains.

Mast Enterprises,
265 North Fourth Street, # 616,
Coeur D'Alene,
ID 83814
Tel: 208 772 8213

Mountain Ark Trader,
PO Box 3170,
Fayetteville,
AR 72701
Tel: 800 647 8909
Fax: 501 442 7191
Suppliers of grains and 100%
buckwheat noodles, Japanese-
style silken tofu, soy milk and
rice milk.

Walnut Acres Organic Farms,
Penns Creek,
PA 17862
Tel: 800 433 3998
Fax: 717 837 1146

Books

Brostoff, Dr Jonathan, and Gamlin, Linda. *The Complete Guide to Food Allergy and Intolerance*, Bloomsbury Publishing

Houlton, Jane. *The Allergy Survival Guide*, Vermilion

Drs Lewith, G, Kenyon, J, and Dowson, D. *Allergy & Intolerance – A complete Guide to Environmental Medicine*, Green Print Press

Magazines

Many publications on health and fitness or on food carry regular articles on diet and food intolerance. *Here's Health* and *Vegetarian Living* are particularly good. *The Inside Story on Food & Health* (5 Lawn Road, London NW3 2XS; subscription £29.95 per annum) is a quarterly magazine dealing with dietary problems – articles, recipes, product information, etc.

Index

Fennel and haddock soup 8
Fish cakes 18
Fish pie with apple 22
Flapjacks 103
Fruit cake 106

Gazpacho 7
Gingerbread 105
Gluten-free pastry 108
Gooey chocolate mousse 96
Gram flour pastry 118
Gram flour sponge cake 115
Gravy 34
Guacamole 15

Indian lentils with sunflower
    seeds 72

Jerusalem artichoke and Brussels
    sprout purée 89

Lemon or orange cake 104
Lemon shortbread 119
London pie 31

Marinated fried tofu 12
Mixed vegetables with carrot
    and onion purée 71
Moussaka 37
Mushroom and nut risotto 55
Mushroom and sunflower seed
    flan 62

Mushrooms stuffed with smoked
    mussels 11

No-butter brandy butter 93

Oat bread 109
Oat pastry 107
Okra and potato stew 70
Orange or lemon cake 104

Pasta primavera 43
Pasta with fresh salmon and
    spinach 24
Pasta with tomato and ham
    sauce 25
Penne paesana 48
Peperonata 84
Pepper, nut and tofu stir-fry 67
Pineapple chicken 42
Pork and parsnip bake 41
Potato and polenta bake with
    apple sauce 52
Potato, leek and apple pie 61

Quinoa and cashew stuffing 35

Raisin muffins 114
Red cabbage and apple
    casserole 54
Rice 'bread' sauce 36
Rice, chilli and bamboo shoot
    casserole 65

Rice with apricots 74
Roast turkey 32
Root vegetable casserole 60
Runner bean and avocado
    salad 81

Smoked mackerel and tofu
    quiche 20
Soya milk shake 100
Spiced rice with green peas and
    pumpkin seeds 73
Spinach and mint salad with
    avocado 79
Spinach soufflé 68
Stir-fried Brussels sprouts 83

Stir-fries 44
Stuffed courgettes (zucchini) 77
Summer fruit and nut crisp 99

Tuna stir-fry 19
Turkey or chicken risotto 27
Turkey, roast 32

Veal or beef à la mode 30
Vegetable stock (bouillon) 2
Victorian salad of warm spring
    vegetables 80

Wholemeal brown loaf 110

The Sensitive Gourmet

Antoinette Savill

If you thought that avoidance of wheat, gluten or dairy products meant you could never again entertain with style or enjoy wonderful food – think again! *The Sensitive Gourmet* contains over 100 mouthwatering, contemporary recipes and menus for every occasion – from family celebrations to summer barbecues.

Using the healthiest and freshest of ingredients, Antoinette Savill has made sure that if you, or one of your family, is among the increasing number of people suffering from food intolerances, you will rediscover the joy of cooking and eating delicious, health-giving food.

Antoinette Savill has been a professional cook and cookery writer for the past 22 years. Following surgery in 1992 she developed multiple food allergies, but has determined not to let illness prevent her enjoyment of good food and entertainment.

Erica White's Beat Candida Cookbook

Containing over 300 easy-to-follow recipes and a 4-point plan to help you recover from candidiasis.

Erica White's Beat Candida Cookbook contains all the help you need to overcome the effects of yeast-related health problems associated with an overgrowth of Candida albicans – chronic fatigue, aching joints and muscles, thrush, IBS to name but a few.

Her 4-point plan shows you how to:

- Stave the yeast by diet
- Boost your immune system with vitamins and minerals
- Take antifungal supplements
- Re-introduce beneficial bacteria into your system

The anti-yeast recipes contained here help starve Candida to death, and are also a great opportunity to learn about health-building foods.

Erica White is a qualified Nutrition Consultant with a successful practice in Leigh-on-Sea, England. This book arose out of her personal experiences of fighting Candida, and has helped restore the health of thousands.

Cooking Without

Barbara Cousins

Cooking Without is not only a collection of delicious and simple recipes, but it is also a book about health: how to gain it and how to keep it.

The book encourages you to build health by eating the right kinds of food at regular intervals. This enables the body to produce extra energy that it can then use to eliminate toxins, reduce weight and heal itself naturally.

The recipes all contain ingredients which are health-promoting, without high levels of salt, fat, sugar or ingredients which cause allergic reactions in many people, such as dairy produce, gluten and yeast.

Barbara Cousins is a nutritional therapist and originally wrote *Cooking Without* for her clients. Self-publishing her work, it has achieved phenomenal success.

Cleanse Your System

Amanda Ursell

The digestive system can be badly affected by our modern lifestyles: stress and the wrong foods all take their toll on our well being. The digestive tract has almost as many nerve endings as the brain, and cleansing the system is both a physiological and psychological process.

Cleanse Your System explains how the digestive system works, and suggests ways to prevent illness and prepare the body for a healthy detox. Unlike other books which often contain starvation diets and quick-fixes, this book encourages a safe and healthy regime to ensure that a healthy balance is restored.

Top nutritionist Amanda Ursell is the author of several health titles. She writes the *Diet Watch* column in the *Sunday Times* and regularly appears on GMTV.